Dr. Katie Evans

Unfortunate Hero

The Soldier's Path From
Trauma and Addiction

ISBN: 1452823707
ISBN-13: 9781452823706
Library of Congress Control Number: 2010905743

About the Author

Katie Evans, Ph.D., CADCIII, CDP, NCACII, is CEO of Dr. Katie Evans, Inc., in Beaverton, Oregon. She co-owns this corporation with her husband SFC Michael L. Kelley (retired). Dr. Evans has a master's degree and a Ph.D. in clinical psychology from Canella University. She has taught as adjunct faculty at Portland State University and several local community colleges. Dr. Evans has worked as a therapist with dual-disordered individuals since 1984. She has published and co-authored numerous articles and five previous books for Guilford Publication, including *Dual Diagnosis: Counseling the Mentally Ill Substance Abuser*, which is now in its second edition. The *Treating Addicted Survivors* book has been translated into Japanese. Dr. Evans continues to travel in Europe, Asia, and the United States giving workshops and keynote addresses on mental health, addiction, and dual-diagnosis-related topics. She was honored to be one of the keynote speakers at the first Northern European Conference on Dual Diagnosis in Sweden, Dr. Evans presented topic was "Treating Addicted Survivors of Trauma."

Dr. Evans wrote *Understanding Post Traumatic Stress Disorder*, second edition, for the Hazelden Foundation and is the primary author for the majority of the Co-Existing Disorder Series. She contributed to the recent edition of their client workbook DVDs in the "Co-Occurring Disorders Series," discussing current practice and research for universities, clinicians, and family members. She is semi-retired, and due to writing and training, she keeps a very small clinical practice in her home office.

Dr. Evans's genuine personality and sense of humor is a gift the makes her style effective with addicted adolescents and adults who suffer denial and is unmotivated for recovery. Dr. Evans has conducted many state and international workshops speaking on co-occurring disorders. Dr. Evans advanced clinical skills are in counseling individuals with both trauma and addiction home study courses. These workshops/home study courses are powerful, demonstrate fresh clinical approaches, and offer materials for both counselors and clients, including worksheets for client teaching and learning strategies on engaging adolescence in recovery, as well as issues common to military families. She has provided services to DODs on evaluating teen drug problems.

Dr. Evans has been a trainer and consultant to the U.S. Department of Veterans Affairs on dual diagnosis and post-traumatic stress disorder and addictions since the mid 1980s. In 1992, Dr. Evans toured military bases working with the Department of Defense educational program in the Pacific Rim. Eight military bases in Japan that were being trained on working with oppositional, sexually abused, and other hurt, angry, and defiant youths hosted her. Her books and other materials are approved for continuing education for most professionals in most states and many countries.

Dr. Evans resides in Oregon with her husband Michael Kelley. He served his country for twenty-two years in the armed forces during both war and peacetime. Dr. Evans has worked with soldiers and their families for many years.

Additional information regarding Dr. Evans's continuing education studies can be found on her website, www.drkatieevans.com; feel free to contact her there.

Table of Contents

Dedication

"This book is dedicated to those who gave their all, in military service for our country. I hope, for some of you, that this book illuminates a path for safety and sobriety on your way home."

The love and support of my spouse, Sergeant First Class Michael L. Kelley (retired), made this workbook possible. A special thanks to another hero, my stepson, Army Specialist Brandon R. Kelley, who served in Operation Iraqi Freedom. Specialist Kelley found hope for sobriety and healing through the integrated recovery model for PTSD and addiction contained in this book. All heroes experience a spiritual journey on their path. To all who read this book, may you know and grow one day at a time.

This book is the culmination of integrating what I know works from years of helping other addicted survivors with new information unique to the addicted soldier survivor. In the final moments of his life at age seventy-seven, my father shared his fifty-two-year history of having nightmares that were never discussed or treated. To him, Army Master Sergeant John T. Jordan, World War II (deceased): May your pain from storming the beach of Normandy help guide me in spirit to serve and offer healing for those who still suffer. I love and miss you, Dad.

Katie Evans, Ph.D.

The Unfortunate Hero

The Unfortunate Hero feels lost and alone,
No map can lead him on the old path home.
Once he was a father, a husband, and a son;
Transformed into "a soldier," a warrior with a gun.
On the fields of battle, he saw the gates to hell;
On the phone with family, he dare not tell;
The old family life seems so far away;
Stoically torn into pieces that smoldering hot day.
"We love you," spoken with quivering voice trying
not to cry,
Ambivalent soldier is torn by duty, honor, and family ties.
"Don't ask, don't tell," he could not share his heavy heart;
"No telling this day's truth—hello, today my friend was
blown apart."
Knowing his loved ones were filled with fear,
He lied to them. "Things are fine. I love you, dear."
What good would come from causing stress to
those at home?
Our soldier has a distant stare; he appears lost and alone.
Splintered by the conflict, will he find a safe and
sober path home?
Drinking and drugs often sought to stop nightmares
and rage;
The addicted soldier survivor now trapped in an
invisible cage.

Katie Evans, Ph.D.

Foreword

A Retired Soldier's Story

I grew up in an abusive home and would be called names and was belittled every day. I loved my family regardless of what they could dish out to me. My childhood through high school was dealing with people who made fun of me except for the few who cared about people. I went to church and learned that God was the only friend I could always trust. I also learned that God would answer prayers only if I gave it totally to God and did not dwell on them. When I stressed about anything, God and I would go to places that were safe and enjoyable. Sometimes it would take someone to nudge me to bring me out of the safe and enjoyable place, back to the cruel reality of the world. I was told over and over again that "sticks and stones may break my bones, but names will never hurt me." My belief that it was true helped me survive the name calling so I would be a better person. "Treat others the way you would like to be treated," was one of the other things that became very important to survival.

Prior to my graduation from high school, I had taken the Armed Forces Entrance Exam. A good score allowed this small-town boy to be an aeronautics engineer working on aircraft for the army. After the graduation, I was on his way to the Military Basic Training Base. When getting off the bus at the training base, I had that familiar feeling of being back home as a young child. I completed the training as an infantryman and was proud of whom I had become and being able to tolerate the name-calling and being treated lower than dirt for nine weeks. I was one buff, tough soldier who was, in my mind, unstoppable.

When I arrived at my first unit of assignment, I was ready for treatment the same way as in the basic training. I was processed in and assigned to a platoon. The platoon sergeant told me to relax, have a seat, and watch some television while he was getting things together for final processing. This was my new family. They treated me with respect and love and I was the look-up-to guy.

After years of being the infantryman, expert at being a soldier, and learning that I was better qualified for aircraft maintenance, I would be of more use after I got out of the military. I became an airplane mechanic who would become the expert at rigging aircraft and one of the few certified to do taxi and run up without a pilot. Years passed by as I had accrued many flight hours and experience being a crewmember and even getting to fly and land the airplanes.

My pride and expertise did not go unnoticed when it came time for a change to the way the military did business. The Army went to contracting the maintenance out. I was devastated because I was the best aviation mechanic and leader the Army had. The contractors asked me to train their people to be as good as I was. "No way am I going to teach my tricks to someone that took my job away," I said. After a couple of days, I was meeting with the commander and told me I would teach them (contractors) what they needed to know. I did not want to have to train the people, but after spending days and weeks training the new hires, I started to enjoy teaching. I enjoyed teaching so much that I would spend time at schools sharing my experiences as a soldier in uniform.

After contractors took over, I was out of the airplane business; I was going to work as a helicopter mechanic and would become the expert on all aspects of the systems.

I would work closely with the contractors who would program certain systems so that when in the field I would be able to fix things on the spot. I would sign off the work that the contractor usually did, and my boss would counsel me about doing the contractor's work on the aircraft. Knowing that survival was important, I would continue to learn from the contractor and become the expert.

The Gulf War had started, and I was on my way home to bury my father-in-law. After several weeks away and then returning to my unit, I felt abandoned and alone because my unit had deployed without me. Eventually I got orders to deploy. I was going to war after several weeks of waiting. I knew I was going to join my unit at war, only to be very disappointed to find that this would not be the case. They assigned me to a unit that treated me as an outsider, but welcomed my experience, willingness to be part of the team, and will to learn and teach new tricks. I saw much devastation while at war, but nothing I could not handle. When the war was over, I ran into my home unit and talked to the higher-ups about going back with them instead of having to go back Stateside with this other unit. After the higher-ups talked to each other, I was going home with my unit and family. As I watched everybody receive his or her awards and decorations, I wished I would receive mine at the same time. Abandoned all over again! Months had passed since the war, and I received an envelope from the unit I was attached during the war, containing a Letter of Appreciation. Just touching it would make it turn to ash, as I was part of the team that received their bronze stars. Abandoned all over again!

A year or so later I was working in an administrative job that required tracking all vehicle and aircraft status. I would ensure that no matter what was required to make the items fully mission capable, I would go beyond the call of duty to make it happen. I would call the depots in the States to inquire about parts available in the system. If not available in the system, I would contract with the manufacturer to have the parts made and delivered. I would receive an ass chewing for getting the part by going outside the box. Shortly after, I would get praise for getting the parts in order to get the aircraft/vehicle back up to operational status, with a wink, "Don't do it again." Whatever it took to get the job done was what made the commanders look good, because their equipment was staying fully mission capable. My boss and I took the heat from the general, who was a real person who put his pants on the same way and truly loved and cared for each soldier as his own children.

A new war was started in Bosnia, and I deployed again doing the same job ensuring that the units received what they needed to support their equipment. I had to go into areas not secured because we were looking for locations for units to set up as they arrived in country. We stopped in a town, devastated by war, and could see no movement or smoke, just bombed-out buildings and houses. Even the railroad tracks had been damaged. The electrical towers were lying on the ground, of no use to anyone. We stopped on the railroad tracks, which were a good place to stop for lunch, as we could watch 360 degrees from our location for any danger that might approach.

Shortly after stopping, we saw movement. It was twenty-six children; the oldest girl was sixteen and the oldest boy was eleven. The children had not had parents around for months, and the sixteen-year-old took the responsibility to care for all the children left behind. The abandonment of children is something I would never understand. The interpreter asked several questions of the children to learn they had no means of staying warm other than gathering in a room huddling with each other. The day was Christmas Eve with eighteen inches of snow. Knowing that they would not have Christmas, as I knew it, caused me to tear up. There were four grown men in the vehicle, and after giving rations to the kids and seeing the precious looks of thanks, it caused us to all cry. Each of the children had tears of love and appreciation for us, as we had helped them with a warm meal that was good and would provide comfort for their tummies for a while.

I decided that when I retired, God would be in charge and I would someday help take care of God's children. I would ensure that children would receive the things God wants them all to have. I got a good job after I retired and was on a mission to save some money to be able to help those children. I injured myself while on the job and learned I would never work again. I was married twice while on active military duty. In both cases my ex-wives betrayed my trust and involved themselves in multiple affairs. The infidelity, which can be common in military life, was brought to my attention by my children. My wife at the time made no attempt to hide her sexual flings. The children told me to divorce her. My fear of losing my children and sense of worthlessness made getting a divorce seem too overwhelming. After finding my wife and her lover with her in my own bed one day I drew the line. I had promised God till death do we part when we married. Both God and I knew I felt very lonely as if. I was dying inside. I kept praying. A nonstop dialogue with God.

Divorce papers were filed. I moved up the Pacific Northwest to be closer to my aging parents. My own children were now adult's with their own children and lives. After moving to the Northwest I found I missed being married. I wanted to find a woman whom I could trust. Trust had now become a larger hurdle in my life than ever before after two failed marriages. I prayed about this issue. Even in the worst of times God has always answered my prayers one of three ways: Yes, No, or Wait. My answer was, "Wait, she is out there." I am thankful that God had given me a couple of extra years to spend with my mother, who was very ill. If I had not had the time for God to work with me on my issues of distrust, I might have missed out on the miracle he had planned for me. I held onto my faith and knew that God does work through us. I had cut back on my drinking, but not yet stopped. I had a spiritual program through my individual relationship with a God of my understanding

I worked for the fiber-optics company that served Oregon. One day I got call saying this woman had a late call and needed, as an emergent situation. She lived alone and worked out of her home. She had already called us twice in the last week, after her telephone lines had been cut, and her computer router had been damaged.

I agreed to stay late. When I rang the doorbell, I saw a shining smile on the face of the woman who opened the door, I could hear God's whisper, "She is the one." Katie Evans opened the door. Katie likes to laugh and say she bought me for $39.95 a month unlimited phone and fiber repair. She was being attacked by identity theft. Her phone lines were cut and her Internet did not work; she had been hacked and her Identification had been stolen. Katie's parents are from the South. She was told by her mother that the way to a man's heart was through his stomach. This was a very different philosophy than my previous wife who thought sex was the way to lasso a man into marriage.

Katie fed me dinner as I stayed late to fix her computer. We talked of fear, faith, trust, and God. She shared her story of recovery from addiction with me. Katie had not drank for 24 years. Each night we talked of strong belief that God had a plan for us. She quoted a book from A.A. that states "nothing ever happens in our lives by mistake. Our friendship turned to a deep spiritual love. Given my Irish background, Katie said, "If we are going to date, I need you to abstain from all drinking." I haven't had a drink in four years or smoked in three years.

So I waited until I was shown the right person to have in my life. I found her, and I am married to the most understanding and wonderful person in the world. She shares the same goal in taking care of God's children. Without her in my life, I believe that I might have perished because of the infection I had after my surgery. I was so sick that I could not even get up to take care of myself or call for help.

Without knowing God in my life as a young child, I would have been very alone and afraid. Because I had God as my soul supporter, I will continue to live life as a child of God. I am constantly looking for ways to help the soldiers who have served in our wars, regardless if they served one day or years. Any soldier of the United States military is a soldier of God by giving their all for their country. Believe in YOUR God with all your heart, be true to him, and your life will be one of love and abundance. Think of God every time you take in a breath, and you will know he is in you, as each breath brings new life to your mind, body, and spirit.

Thank you to all my brothers and sisters, soldiers and civilians who so selflessly supported our wars at home and abroad. We need each other and God if we are to survive and healed to feel like the fortunate soldier, blessed in so many ways.

—Michael L. Kelley (Army Retired)

Overview and Preface

I wrote this book for both our soldiers and the counselors and other helpers who work with returning military personnel suffering trauma and addiction. Many military survivors have read and used this material themselves and have found great relief. Their emails and notes to me are very special. Our soldiers are "unfortunate heroes" who stepped up and joined the ranks of the military to keep us safe. They came home to changed people and a changed world and realized how much they too had changed since the day they deployed. These veterans are finding that they need support for that transition, although they do not always want it or know how to find the help that best suits their needs. I wrote this book to honor and offer them and their loved ones hope, support, and symptom relief. This book offers a model for a new life.

It was witnessing the pain and struggle of the addicted soldier survivor to achieve and maintain dual recovery that led me to write this new addition to my PTSD and addiction publications. The tears and years I have shared with veterans and other survivors with PTSD and addiction have taught me much. I say to my peers (addiction and trauma professionals), we must be prepared to intervene and teach skills for treating flashbacks and memories that escalate addiction and have, to date, impeded recovery for many soldiers.

Many addicts and alcoholic survivors of trauma lose hope when their recovery attempts "fail," escalating the synergism of relapse, hopelessness, pain, and survivor guilt. The rage imploding in the soldier with PTSD and addiction has led to a 40% increase in suicides, a 67% increase in violent crimes/deaths, and a 56% increase in head injuries from

2006 to 2007. Many of these statistics I share are found at www.military.com and in other periodicals. I have found that the numbers do change in that military. Families have many secrets and the "need to know" rule is stringent.

The nightly news grossly underreports statistics and facts, as many of these statistics and facts are "classified" and not available to anyone who is outside the family or does not have the appropriate clearance. The inability to discuss what is being seen and done has a profoundly isolating effect on the soldier. This adds to survivor guilt, a symptom of post-traumatic stress disorder, which is a diagnosis common to the suffering soldier and his or her family. Even if the soldier feels it is safe to discuss some of what he or she did and saw while deployed, the soldier fears the reaction to the telling of the story. The soldier does not want to upset loved ones who also are already traumatized by fear for the safety of their loved one.

When the over 525,000 soldiers return from Iraqi Freedom and the other two million soldiers return from other campaigns, we will be unable to address their social and health problems with the already overloaded and underfunded Veterans Administration (VA).

There are but a few professionals adequately trained and equipped to intervene, engage, and appropriately treat these addicted spiritually and physically wounded warriors. I have provided consultation and training to the VA for twenty-four years. The special issues related to the addicted soldier survivor require a model for treatment and curriculum. This workbook provides both a dual recovery model and much-needed client curriculum in order for us to have access to a model that has already been successful in treating many wounded soldiers.

The U.S. VA has referenced my book, *Treating Addicted Survivors of Trauma* (1995, co-authored by J. Michael Sullivan, Ph.D.). I have expanded on our five-stage model for addiction and trauma recovery to address issues unique to the wounded warrior.

I have tried to create a clear yet comprehensive treatment and recovery model that begins with this client/counselor workbook.

My research of conversion experiences in my 1998 dissertation, along with the strength of survivors, has kept me inspired to keep listening and learning improved methods for offering help to dual-disordered individuals. I hope my work of these past thirty-five years continues to assist and support both counselors and their clients in a painful journey toward dual recovery, leading them to a new improved life that was once nearly destroyed.

This workbook is the center point where education about dual recovery begins. Family members, soldiers, and treatment providers will benefit from reading and using this workbook. Specific exercises are included to assist in the healing of the wounds of PTSD-related trauma, head injuries, and coexisting addiction.

Chapter 1

PTSD: What Is Post-Traumatic Stress Disorder?

Post-traumatic stress disorder (PTSD) is a "normal response to an abnormal situation," according to the DMS-IVR (the book used to diagnosis mental and emotional disturbances). In many ways, PTSD does not belong in the DSM-IVR, as it is a comprehensive set of symptoms that meets the definition of having a true medical problem. However, at the time of this writing, we are still using mental health over medical diagnostics. What is important, if you are a victim of this disorder, is that you begin to understand that the strange, angry, depressed, and even explosive outbursts you now have are due to psychological distress that is most likely a result of deployment. You and hundreds of thousands of other individuals stepped up and left normal civilian non-wartime duties, honoring our country with military service. What you did not expect was to be suffering from PTSD, a normal reaction to what you saw and experienced as part of your military tour of duty.

Many soldiers turn to alcohol and other drugs to numb the pain of PTSD. Substance abuse leads to a path of double-trouble, making recovery from PTSD or addiction impossible without integrated treatment of the two disorders in a simultaneous approach. To go to one group, learn the symptoms of PTSD, then go to another group, and learn about the disease of addiction can be helpful. However, my experience has been that unless we teach our hero survivors how to sleep without getting high or drunk, and do so in the same class or group at the same time, the outcome for safety and sobriety is poor. It is imperative that the therapist and the client understand how and why drinking and using other drugs further aggravate Polytrauma (physical loss of limbs, sight) and make symptoms of PTSD and head injuries worse not better. We need to provide a simple, logical, and helpful model that shows the survivor why chemical abuse creates more brain trauma and how what seems like an escape can become a prison of problems.

Explaining what else works faster than drinking or using drugs for relief of psychological or emotional numbing is the only strategy that has any chance of success for dual recovery. Again, simultaneous integrated treatment is necessary for coexisting disorders.

Military Recovery Model for Polytrauma PTSD and Addiction

Trauma, Trust, Treatment

Stage I: Crisis Intervention
Goal: Safety
Therapeutic engagement, pre-treatment, trusts building, teaching skills to stop flashbacks and trauma reenactments. Contracts for sobriety and safety. Case management.

Stage II: Building Stage
Goal: Skills Learning
Teach boundary setting, assertiveness, skills for emotional wound care and affect containment.

Stage III: Education Stage
Goal: Reframing
Empowerment, not victim survivor, building learned recovery skills

Stage IV: Integration
Goal: Weave Past and Present
Reducing shame, shift from fear-based to faith-based thinking, intimacy issues addressed with family.

Stage V: Maintenance
Goal: Ongoing Recovery
Living life on life's terms, trigger management, ability to ask for help, no longer a victim, and survivor skills, now thriving in dual recovery.

Safety First The crisis stage goals described above are common to most individuals. The goal is to help the soldier/survivor to feel stable and safe. Stopping the use of chemicals and/or clearing all addictive chemicals from our bodies are difficult but important first steps. Detox is not easy. The symptoms of detox vary from one user to another and how much and what type of drugs each was using. You may relapse. Do not give up on yourself. It is progress not perfection.

The five-stage model revealed in this book works! (Evans, K & Sullivan 1990, 1995, 2001.) My former colleague J.M. Sullivan and I developed some of these suggestions together. This book reviews successful treatment that leads to long-term dual recovery. Following his 2001 retirement, I continued to expand, change, and replace ideas previously discussed in our earlier publications. Those suffering from addiction and coexisting PTSD improved at a faster rate. This book is built from the initial five-stage recovery model published.

It is sometimes easy to overlook the obvious. In 1998 I completed my dissertation at my Ph.D. program on what motivates addicted survivors to change. (Katie Evans Library of Congress 1998.) In 1983, understanding why I could no longer drink made it much easier to stop drinking. The "just say no" method, to stop the use of mood-altering chemicals, works on children ages five to nine. The big campaign to use this motto in the 1980s turned out ultimately to have no positive impact on youth eleven and older. I have evaluated more than one heavily marijuana-drugged thirteen-year-old wearing a "Just Say No" T-shirt from DARE.

Children listen to some degree to their parents. They do not want Mom or Dad angry with them, and they do not want to get into trouble. By the onset of adolescence, however, the ugly head of rebellion pops up along with frequent middle-fingers and oppositional defiant behavior begins. In other words, if you tell an adolescent no, the adolescent is more likely to do the opposite. Tell a teen something is good for them, and they will not do it. This is the normal developmental mindset of preteen and teen development. There are normal phases of childhood, including adolescents, and adulthood. The surly confused behavior in a child with no PTSD is a long-lasting final step needed them to separate from their parents.

Many enlistees in the military are teenagers. Even if they do not suffer the additional immaturity common to drug users whose emotional development stopped at the age they began to use drugs, they are still teens. I have interviewed many soldiers who acknowledged that they left a "crazy home life" by enlisting. They expected to have the rules bent and broken to suit their desires—an attitude of enlistment or enrollment like high school football. They found, however, that "no" meant "no" with your new "Uncle" Sam. Many youths, trying to rebel with their new parents (the military) against their real parents, inform the latter of their enlistment only after the papers are signed.

Later they discover that joining the military is not like quitting the football team. You can't get a letter from your mother saying, "Please send my son out Iraq, it is too hot for him there and he doesn't really like the people in the Army. He is ready to come home now." The military becomes the new parent. The military has a firm set of rules making them the provider of structure. Enlistment into a highly structured system, providing the structure the young adult needed from parents, is now firmly in place. The lack of personal accountability, disrespect for authority, and entitlement are a recipe given to the daughter or son. We have spoiled a whole generation of youth with too much stuff and too little concern for others or the respect for authority and the laws of our society. Parents trying to get an attorney to circumvent the military's protocol without good reason are not helpful to anyone.

Many parents will see an adult come home after boot camp. Children become proud of their own achievements. They are honorable men and women soldiers beginning their emotional emancipation from a formerly "pothead kid" to a healthier, more mature adult. This is done in the military, at the beginning of service, not after discharge when the damage is done.

For counselors and clients alike, one place that might help lessen the scars of war is further training on adolescent development, the stress of adolescence. Boot camp leaders would benefit from knowledge of life-span and mental health issues and the skills to manage and offer emotional emancipation from Mom and Dad, which is offered in a terrifying style for many. Their new military family trains successful developmental skills, thus preventing the fragmented survivor from suffering mental health issues and/or dishonorable discharge when feeling like he or she can no longer cope. Solutions are offered at the beginning and miracles happen daily.

Talking/Texting = Ambivalence and Mental Meltdowns

Who would have considered that more contact with your deployed loved ones could be causing additional damage to soldiers and the ones they love? Sadly, research and anecdotal information has revealed to us some mistakes that, as you read this book, most likely continue to occur. For officers and those stationed with teleconferencing, modern modems are very direct way to worry young wives, mothers, and children.

However, in this new millennium of battle and high technology, we have found that soldiers and families can have nearly instant access to information through text messaging, cell phones, and email. While under certain conditions this is not always true, it is truer now than at any other time of war. Use of this technology is proving to be more damaging to the mental health of many soldiers, as they have had more contact home with their spouses and families than in any other war. Now, at first glance, keeping such close touch with family might seem like a good idea. Unfortunately, for many soldiers, it has created ambivalence. A huge tug-of-war exists in the hearts and heads of all of those who are deployed. Frequent phone calls with family reminds them how much they are missed and needed at home.

The increased contact among spouses, parents, and children has led soldiers to feel more displaced, torn between the distractions of being away from home and being a part of the new military family. If text messaging and phone calls are done in a hysterical moment without thinking of the soldier circumstance, it added to the feeling of being torn in half. This feeling of being torn in half is referred to as ambivalence. This incredible ambivalence, feeling torn apart by the love and needs of the family with those of the role of a soldier, has led to increased acuity in symptoms of PTSD.

In previous wars, the military had to limited phone contact to emergencies due to phone access for emergency use only. Mail was the main source of contact from home. In letter writing, most people are more thoughtful. As a wife or parent wrote to the soldier, they would be more thoughtful and less selfish in what was written. In a letter, the soldier also was more thoughtful of the impact of what he wrote would have on a wife or mother. The letters were focused on mutual love and support. Ambivalence showed itself through the instant gratification of having contact and attempts to fill that hole inside left by the loved one's absence. These types of communications have led to an increase of infidelity and even divorce, The aftermath of the emotional, guilt-ridden accounts maybe emailed when the writer was intoxicated and increased by instant email and phone calls from loved ones has been so frequent that soldiers have felt torn apart. They never feel as if they are in the right place at the right time. How can they focus on being soldiers if their spouses are calling, now with cell phones and texting, to share emotional "what about me" day-to-day feelings of being overwhelmed without their spouses help with the children or yard work? ("Infidelity and its effects," Vandevoorde, S: 2006. *Separated by Duty United by Love.*)

The positive effect of brainwashing and isolation the military uses to create "a soldier" begins to erode, and the soldier falls apart with too much contact from loved ones. Soldiers are not isolated enough to focus on the war. They feel as if they should be home, while at the same time, they know they should be soldiers. The "Where should I be?" question has led to further questions, such as, "Where do I belong?" and "Who am I?" All of these unhelpful questions lead people to feel torn apart. It is as if they have to have the answer to a true/false test, but the question isn't true and false. They feel lost, confused, vulnerable, and prone to trance states, and become more traumatized. I am not blaming anyone or anything for this eventuality. It is simply a fact. In addition, head injuries affect a person's ability to manage extreme emotions. The loved one writing or calling has not yet seen the effects of head trauma on a person. It would be most helpful to educate family members prior to the soldiers return about the specific effects of a brain injury. The more emotion in a conversation the more troubeling it is for a damaged brain to understand the content and any nuences of a conversation. If as a wife I knew this, I would not bring up intensly feeling, or fact based conversations in text mail. A letter thoughtfully written and perhaps aided by the help of a counselor knowledgeable about head injuries could prevent a great deal of hurt, rage and perhaps divorce.

The Vietnam War was the first televised war. Americans at home, not in the military, saw the reality of war—horror, death, and dismemberment. It was the televising of the Vietnam War that led to such a strong antiwar movement at home. However well meaning we were, we became anti-soldier not antiwar. Vietnam vets were called "baby killers," something the celebrated heroes of other wars did not suffer.

The damage from this was so overwhelming that many vets still suffer confusion from being drafted (not enlisting) into a war they did not believe was right, only to come home and be hated for going. This mixed message has resulted in a lot of trance states and confusion. A damaging trance belief is trauma induced. Most often in an intense state of fear, anger and confusion. The repetitions of a trance statement believe is like taping the message to the front of a mirror. Each time the person looks into the mirror they see this trance state. Enacting symptoms of dissociation, Flashbacks and other trauma based symptoms.

In many ways our entire country suffered symptoms of PTSD from the Vietnam War. On 911 our country and the people who enjoy our freedoms here realized that the peace time safety that we enjoy were attracted and forever changed by terrorism. In New York, Washington D.C. were once a vacation destination now hold horrific memories of what and who we lost that day.

In the current Middle East conflict, we now know to honor and celebrate our soldiers serving in the military, protecting us, even if we hate the war.

We owe the unfortunate hero's more than a medal or "Thank you." The high levels of ambivalence, dissociation trance state are only some of the symptoms that require our funding for their help, disability and retraining to a new life, as a matter of compassion and honor.

The symptoms of PTSD from the Iraqi conflict are as destructive as those of Vietnam. It is only the s amount of ambivalence that is different. The frequent emails and phone calls from home have hindered soldiers from being able to focus on their military world. The soldier best chance of survival is to become part of a different family—the military—than the one left behind.

Change is not easy. The struggle lies in making the decision about what is the "right" thing to do. Our quick contacts about the daily frustrations of life with our loved ones through has led to a decreased awareness on the part of family members about the effect their words of despair have on their soldiers. This is a phenomenon unique to the current military campaign.

Post-Traumatic Stress Disorder (PTSD)

PTSD refers to a set of symptoms and problems that can develop after a traumatic event. So intensely frightening and dangerous is the traumatic event, that we experience psychological and physiological terror. This level of stress, if prolonged, develops a type of imprinting in our hard wiring—our brain. There is research that shows that individuals with PTSD have a very different brain scan result than those individuals who do not have PTSD. However, these specialized brain scans are not worth the time and cost, because as you keep reading this workbook, a part of you will know if you, in fact, suffer from PTSD as a result of your military service and/or other trauma. If, before entering the military, you had already had a traumatic experience, then you are suffering from what I call "complex military PTSD." If, like many survivors, you are getting drunk or stoned to numb your emotional pain, you now have the dual diagnosis of PTSD and addiction—two problems so intertwined that they require specialized treatment. If you want lasting help for your nightmares and other symptoms of PTSD, you need to get and stay clean and sober. An alcohol- and drug-free life is necessary if you wish to reduce or even eliminate that part of you that "relives" Iraqi Freedom or any other military campaign through flashbacks or nightmares.

During treatment and perhaps afterward, you must abstain from using alcohol and other drugs for numbing out in order to grieve your losses, experience resentment, and receive relief from flashbacks and nightmares in recovery. Getting drunk and high and trying to "just forget about the whole thing" is most likely not working. If you and many others who survived the unimaginable could find the solution at the bottom of a bottle, then there would be no need for drug treatment programs to exist. Nor would there be a reason for me to write or you to read this workbook.

Like many alcoholics, we were seeking fun and relief from our woes when we first began drinking and abusing drugs. If conditions were right, what started as partying started us on the long and troublesome road of addiction. Unlike our nonalcoholic fellows, what we experience is an entirely different set of outcomes from our chemical use. We find a type of instant gratification and euphoria. If we are paying attention, we may also notice that our tolerance to alcohol and other drugs is much higher than our nonalcoholic peers. Genetically, we were born with the ability to drink more and have fewer alcohol-related effects than others. We have to drink more and more to achieve the same desired effect. In drinking more than others drink, we often appear to be sober and drive our nonalcoholic peers home. It seems as if our metabolic tolerance is so high that we have much better physical metabolizing for alcohol.

In fact, the brain chemistry is different for alcoholics. Tolerance, according to research, is the best early predictor of who will be an alcoholic (Altman, Milam). The key issue here is that, during the progression of addiction, not all parts of the body develop tolerance in the same way or at the same time. This is how alcohol overdose occurs. One minute the alcoholic is babbling about something, the next they suffer kidney failure or receptor distress. The disease of addiction is chronic, progressive, and fatal. It keeps getting worse, never better. We begin to progressively develop middle- and late-stage symptoms of alcoholism. What once was the solution to stress—alcohol and other drug use—has now become an additional problem. You now have two intertwining maladies.

To you soldier, the drinking and roughhousing are becoming coiled in a psychotic, dangerous connection. You may think that drinking is the only remedy you have available to numb out bad memories. What I hope you hear loudly is that getting drunk and high is just a detour that leads to another dead-end road. What once was the solution is now the problem. These two diseases are washing out needed brain neurotransmitters, like serotonin, which can lead to developing signs of a third disease, that of anxiety and/or depression. You need serotonin to sleep, relax, and feel hopeful in order to live life one day at a time. It is at this juncture that an expert needs to conduct an evaluation to see if your condition would stabilize sooner if antidepressant medications were used.

The trauma that may have preceded your military experience might include being a victim of robbery or assault or suffering severe deprivation, such as chronic poverty or starvation. You may have been physically, sexually, or emotionally abused as a child. You can even get PTSD from observing a violent accident. You may have grown up with an alcoholic and/or mentally ill parent who said one thing and did another. The symptoms may show up only during a particular situation and be limited in time. Alternatively, they may occur over a long period and in a more generalized fashion. I cannot state this clearly enough, drinking and using is unsafe behavior. You were trained to be a warrior.

A traffic jam or marital riff can explode so fast so far that you will once again suffer that sick lost feeling.

Consider the case of Susan who suffered severe symptoms of PTSD with intense dissociation due to brain washing of another type. For abused children brain washing is sometimes referred to as "grooming." Grooming is how perpetrators gain compliance from their targeted victims by means of "baby steps." In the case of incest, the child is slowly groomed into compliance with the family members over a period of time where small demands to follow directions are made in order to gain control over behavior. For example, "Come sit by me," then "Come sit on my lap," then "Give my neck a massage," then "Give Daddy a kiss," then "Give Daddy a bigger kiss." I think, by this point, you get the main idea about shaping compliance.

Grooming and brainwashing serve several functions in preparing the child to be abused compliantly without yelling or telling. It gives the perpetrator power to direct behavior and achieve compliance. It also leads to blaming the victim for the abuse. I have heard hundreds of perpetrators justify their pedophilia through such statements as, "She seduced me; it is all her fault," or "She never said for me to stop." The child begins to pick up this self-blame either from overt or covert messages given to him or her from the person in positional control. If the perpetrator did not use grooming strategies with the child, then that child would tell someone, scream, yell, or do all the things they wish they could have done years later when they struggle with survivor guilt.

Brainwashing also can be used to reward a child as if the abuse is a sign of "special" love. Trances and confusion follow when the child is told conflicting and ridiculous reasons why "having sex with Daddy" is being a "good girl or boy." The child may be called "a little princess or good little soldier" or told, "You are so special." The child may learn that compliance earns him or her praise. Obviously, any child wants to feel loved and adored. In this type of abuse, children also are developing cognitive and emotional conflicts, causing them to feel hurt, guilty, and confused. This scenario creates a double bind and trance state and, as the child develops into an adult, he or she is distrusting and confused about the difference between love and sex. If being raped or sodomized by a family member is such a "special thing," why is a child told to never tell anyone about his or her "little secret"?

Susan's offender had abused her sexually and physically from the age of three to nine. Susan had been groomed with intermittent reinforcement so she believed it was all her fault. This creates the symptom of "survivor guilt." Susan had been brainwashed to believe that her parents would divorce, she could be sent away, the police would come and put her dad in prison, or any or all of these things would occur if Susan told someone about their little secrets. There is a saying in recovery groups that "you are only as sick as your secrets."

To survive the painful physical act of being raped as a four-year-old, Susan learned how to "go away" or dissociate her mind from her body. Susan used dissociation to forget her childhood. She had almost no memories of her childhood or of the abuse she experienced (amnesia and dissociation). She had always felt different from others, as if she never fit in (estrangement). She had always felt that she was the target of others' criticism and that nothing she did was ever good enough (victim-stance thinking and a pessimistic worldview). Susan's story is one of early childhood abuse by a trusted parent.

Susan immediately entered the military to escape "that house." This coercive type of grooming often is more damaging than being threatened with a knife by a stranger. In the first scenario, the child becomes stuck in an ambivalent world where she had a black-and-white, good-or-bad life reaction. The escaping of her body with her brain is and was a highly dissociative strategy to survive. Over time, Susan's ability to dissociate took on a life of its own. She was no longer aware that she was not paying attention or present in the moment. She would appear to be listening, even answering questions, when, in fact, and she was not mentally present. Due to her heavy use of disassociation, Susan was very suggestible to even subtle demands. The perpetrator and her dissociative state hypnotized her to believe or doubt her own perceptions; thus, she was frequently seeking external support and validation. The need to ask other people what to do can certainly be bothersome. If the question is serious and a person has a potential self-gain in a response, he or she will answer the question differently than a more detached person. The need to ask other people what is the "right thing to do" can lead to further confusion and a sense of helplessness. Be it a man or woman, any time a person has a power relationhip with the victim of abuse, even what seems like consentual affairs. If the perpetrator has rank over the soldier then it is not an equal relationship. MIS is the code for molested in service a topic rarely discussed on CNN. If the soldier feels trapped and quietly survives the trauma or fails to report the abuse, they are blamed. Even loving f family members, the police or the military may seem to blame the victim, by asking questions about the trauma without proper training.

Many people ask, "Am I crazy because I have PTSD?" No! Remember, PTSD refers to a normal response to an abnormal (traumatic) situation.

For those individuals who have preexisting PTSD, who have already begun seeking out drugs or alcohol as a numbing tool or are using dissociation and have begun down the road of complex trauma and addiction, it is my greatest wish that you will read and write in this book and even use a journal as you work to fully disclose those trance states so you can read this with an open mind. No one is judging you or anything you have done to cope with the trauma of life in and out of the military. You have survived! Transcend from survivor to thriver with all your skills and experiences.

You enlisted in the military to be of service to your country. If the recruiter had given you this book to read before enlistment, you might have run as fast and as far away from that recruitment office as possible. You may feel as if the military has betrayed or abandoned you. It may sound embarrassing to state your experience in that manner.

On the other hand, some people develop the adrenaline rush from combat. Their brain chemistry has changed, and some very unsafe behaviors for themselves and others give them the "I am invincible" rush. They survive trauma by becoming a "superhero" who is bigger, stronger, and invincible. The military rewards this behavior and might reframe it as bravery. It can lead to a type of denial where you are no longer able to feel empathy or be sensitive to the hurt or pain of others. This can lead to harsh words, angry fights, and, sadly, the loss of spouse, family, and an angry separation from loved ones.

Over the time you were separated from your family during your deployment or military service, a distance began between you and your own family. Those in the military who are risking their lives and are isolated with you in a "need to know location" become your family. Watching someone who is now family die on the battlefield hurts you as if you had lost a sister or a brother. Sometimes what occurs is "trauma bonding." A reality of coeducation is that now military men and women are together on the battlefield. Surviving desperate situations together can lead to developing a special bond. If boundaries between men and women are soft, this shared pain can be experienced as love. Trauma bonding has led to many divorces. The fear that this could occur is also as destructive. Keep your boundaries strong and understand who you are as you become a soldier. The family chapter will discuss this issue further.

Consider that during your boot camp and every moment since you became a soldier, you have been told, "The military is your mother, your father, your sister, your brother—you are a soldier and nothing else is to interfere with that duty." Many of us outside the military world call this state "as-needed brainwashing," even if it appears to be an extremely rude way to treat a person. The military uses brainwashing as a clear design to save the soldier's life. The civilian does not know the importance of boot camp training. In fact, brainwashing occurs during the prewar training situation.

Chapter 2 will discuss brainwashing and its similarity to grooming in creating psychological conditioning to do what is ordered without debate or questioning so you will survive. Please complete Chapter 1 questions before going on to Chapter 2.

Chapter 1 Questions

If you need more space, write on a separate piece of paper and clip to book.

1. Did you feel confused or ambivalent about your deployment? What made you feel that way?

2. How did the phone or email contact from home make you feel?

3. What do you wish you could have told your family and friends but did not due to concern that they might worry too much?

4. Complete this statement: "I think I have PTSD because sometimes I …"

5. Complete this statement: "I think I had symptoms of PTSD before I joined the military from …"

6. Complete this statement: "My PTSD changed in the military; my symptoms were ..."

7. Complete this statement: "I had secret fears that ..."

8. List three people you trusted before entering the military. Do you still trust them? Why or why not?

9. Record other thoughts or feelings you are experiencing as you consider these questions and read this book.

10. Whom do you see as your family at this time—your parents, spouse, and children, or the military? Has your idea of who your family is changed since before your enlistment? How?

Tips for Counselors

In the back of this book are some inserts to help you help your client and to clarify the recovery model. It is typed out on a one-page chart. It is an excellent tool for individual counseling or to share with a group.

Chapter 2

Military Polytrauma, PTSD, and Addiction

"You have joined the military, soldier, it is all about you!" You may be one of the few people on this planet who never had any type of grief or loss, trauma, or childhood abuse. If so, then the PTSD you are experiencing is strictly from your military life. Your trauma is based on what occurred the moment you became the "property of Uncle Sam." If, in addition, you never abused alcohol or other drugs, you are a miracle. The severity of the military trauma you experienced, how long it continued, and what response you saw from those around you may all contribute to your PTSD. This is especially true concerning the behaviors of senior officers and other authority figures and, most importantly, if you killed the enemy in the line of duty. Taking all of these factors into account can predict if your acute stress will linger into a more prolonged stress anxiety disorder known as PTSD. The duties of a soldier during war are in and of themselves a PTSD experience. What did you see? How long were you there? Did the death, destruction, and mayhem make logical sense in any way? Most likely, the answer is no. Since Desert Storm, and going back as far as Vietnam or even the Civil War, the reasons why young people enlisted were supposed to be related to the protection of our country's freedom, but it wasn't always clear (Grossman. David 2006).

I am now addressing mental health and substance abuse, which is pervasive in those who have served our country. If anything, my pride and gratitude for what you endured so that I could have the freedom even to write this workbook brings tears to my eyes. This is a booklet to begin the healing process from PTSD. Your PTSD may be completely military-caused, or your symptoms may be more severe if you entered the service vulnerable to PTSD from previous life experiences. Let me state for you clearly once again—PTSD is a normal response to an abnormal situation. Understand that, as a soldier, you have been at risk of death from both enemy and "friendly fire" (I do not consider any bullet or rocket headed in my direction as friendly!). The trauma from your military tour will be a combination of your own personal pain and the secondary or vicarious trauma from watching the death or dismemberment of those around you.

Kill or Be Killed

Military brainwashing is necessary for the mission and safety of the soldier. The words "lock and load" have been common to the training of American soldiers since the Civil War. Drills and conditions assist soldiers to successfully load a musket with gunpowder, oilpaper cones, and the ball to prepare for musket fire. *The Warriors*, a book by Glen Gray, discusses the conditions causing exhaustion of Civil War soldiers. Gray states, "With dazed states and terrible conditions, sharp consciousness is lost." Exhaustion to a point of mindlessness leads a soldier to stop thinking and simply survive without conscious thought. The unconscious breeds a highly hypnotizable state of mind when hungry, exhausted, tired, and afraid. Our Civil War soldiers became frozen mentally, physically, and spiritually. At Gettysburg, the slaughter that killed as many young Americans in three days as seven years of the war in Vietnam, 27,574 loaded muskets were recovered and only 12,000 had been fired. The psychology of that war included "brother against brother"; thus, ambivalence undermined brainwashing and conditioning. In studying the Cold Harbor attack of 1864 during the Civil War and the soldiers under Grant's command, it was found that only 10% of the soldiers actually shot to kill. The other 90% either miss-shot above the enemies' heads or joined the chain of loading and passing muskets to those 10% who were standing aiming to kill.

Other studies of the Civil War, as well as World War II, demonstrate that 80–85% of soldiers never shot their guns at the enemy (Marshall). According to Grossman in his book *On Killing*, "The desire to kill after you look into the eyes of another human being and see them as human, leads to the choice to not kill. They are no longer the enemy, they are human beings." Grossman goes on to state in the psychology of military boot camp, "The reluctance of an individual to behave in an aggressive way without any personally strong threat is predictably poor." Boot camp training spends hours training soldiers to arm and load a weapon. Praise is given to those soldiers who rapidly assemble and load their weapons to fire. Sharpshooters are rewarded and specially selected for important missions. What is not discussed, as if it were a military secret, is why only 10% of these marksmen will actually shoot and kill when they look another human in the eye.

For the non-killers, Lord Moran discusses their trauma in the book *Anatomy of Courage*. Moran suffered great emotional trauma after surviving World War I without killing any enemy.

He acknowledged the kills of the men under his command complicated his trauma. He stated that signing a paper certifying that his two hundred men were fit to serve felt like he was signing their death warrants. Moran, a medical officer in World War I, believed that "the healers, the medics" suffered less trauma from war, as they had a job to do and they were heroes on the battlefield. The difference in psychological damage between those who killed and those who helped was significant.

Officers statistically suffer less PTSD than lower-ranking soldiers. They rarely kill the enemy, as their job is to order other lower-level soldiers to kill. They suffer some survivor guilt. However, this type of survivor guilt is far less damaging for them, as they did not have to kill so they were far less afraid.

Glen Gray, driven by his own guilt after the deaths of all the men under his command in the Civil War, confessed, "I am ashamed by my deeds and my nation's deeds, the deeds of humanity; I am ashamed of being a man."

By Vietnam, the firing rate changed from 10% to 90% according to Peter Watson's book, *War in the Mind*. Nowhere in general psychology is the therapist taught to address his or her repugnance toward killing and the refusal to kill. The slaughter of another human is not just "stress" like a hard day at work; it is a cultural conspiracy of morality, forgetfulness, confusion, brainwashing, and the nature of war for thousands of years. The killer is in the nature of each individual man.

Logic and passion collide and military brainwashing fails when it is time to kill. Those who kill count their kill and suffer great survivor guilt. The soldier's ambivalence and self-hatred for following "questionable" orders or defying orders can lead to extreme mental breakdown, according to Glen Gray. The ambivalence around the Vietnam War was so intense it divided the American people into those who would fight and those who headed to Canada.

The psychological trauma was great to the Vietnam vet, who was a 1960s "flower child" dropped in the jungle. Disoriented, tired, hungry, and becoming full of self-hatred can be best captured by stating the destruction of psychological ambivalence. Vietnam destroyed fine men and women who still fill the halls of our VA hospitals, plagued by violent rages, flashbacks, nightmares, and borderline psychosis. They were young men and women who were flooded with psychological and sociological misinformation, confusion, and, yes, ambivalence.

A friend of mine who served in Special Forces in Vietnam told me recently that he had never heard such quietness and felt such fear as that of an airplane load of drafted eighteen- and nineteen-year-olds on their way to their first tour of Vietnam.

Factors in Preparing a Solider to Kill/Boot Camp

Exhaustion inoculation, prepare brainwashing for exhaustion in war.

1. Little to no sleep.
2. Starvation, poor food, or little food.
3. Fight or flight, create hostile training environment emphasizing ongoing exhaustion.

"Abnormal behavior in an abnormal situation is normal behavior" (Victor Frankel, author and Nazi concentration camp survivor).

Unfortunate Hero

Hate and Hatred of the Enemy

Inoculation for brainwashing in all wars includes the use of code names for missions and enemies. For example, in the Civil War we had Yankees and Rebels; in World War II, there were Japs, Jerries, Nips; The Vietnam War dehumanized the enemy with freaks, gooks, Viet Cong; the Gulf War used terrorists, rag heads. The enemy is even referred to as a terrorist cell (like a cancer that will spread and kill us all).

I mention the above only to point out how hate and fear are mental states easily programmed in boot camp. Although it is detrimental to success in battle, this is critical to understand for soldier and therapist to break the fundamental "hate" trance states that keep nightmares, night sweats, and flashbacks alive and destroy our soldiers and everyone who loves them.

Boot camp (and perhaps your childhood) prepares you to kill for "our county" and for the "right reasons." The Twin Towers 9/11 terrorist attack escalated fear and hatred throughout the world, and brave men and women joined the military to serve us and save our homeland.

The beliefs about the politics that led us into Iraq cause a great deal of survival guilt for many nonmilitary nations of civilians. How did we end up sending our troops over to invade a country where there were no weapons of mass destruction? I believe this was a fatal political mistake that cost us the lives of many Americans along with respect for the United States from other citizens of the planet.

Soldiers experience unique trauma in training and in the field. To escape the pain of the trauma, mind-altering substances are often used. For successful treatment, recovery, and trauma-free living, the soldier seeking help must adopt a drug- and alcohol-free lifestyle.

Since the time of the Civil War, our passionate heroes enlisted in the military for their own noble reasons. To take a boy from the family farm and send him off to war required training. To shift from pitching hay to automatic weapons, training was needed. Most important of all, our heroes had to be taught to kill. It is only instinctive to injure or kill another human when one perceives his or her own life or the life of a loved one at risk. The military developed "boot camp" to shape the thinking of our soldiers to kill instinctively. "Kill or be killed" is what the soldiers in training are told. In order to accomplish the task, it requires that we brainwash the worldview of a loving son to that of a warrior/killer. The stages of brainwashing that will later be reviewed are included in the "psychological orientation material," which is at the fingertips of all drill sergeants. It is their job to traumatize an individual into being a killer on command. The motives are to "carry out the mission" and to protect the soldier and his or her fellow soldiers from the enemy. This training introduces them to the survival needed. To deploy without the calm and precise knowledge of how to kill would be certain suicide.

In circumstances where a person is threatened and feels helpless, he or she suffers PTSD. However, their dissociations and trance states are likely related to not only the need to be strong, but also to the necessity to prove to superiors that they are strong. Boot camp is no doubt a rigorous and grueling experience. If you survived your drill sergeant yelling in your face, then you have been converted from a civilian to a soldier. The conditioning at boot camp is done precisely to teach you to automatically respond to a life-threatening situation and to "kill or be killed." Hyper-vigilance and attending closely to your environment are critical if you are to survive. You work out and run for hours in ninety-degree weather to condition your body. You are taught the methods of war and self-defense. During this training, a part of you develops magical thinking, believing that you will never feel victimized again. Sadly, any belief that is formed in childhood and has a magical quality is a trance.

Isaac (not his real name) is a veteran of the Korean War. Before he went to war, Isaac operated heavy equipment for highway construction—everything from powerful bulldozers to precision road graders. After the war, he could run only the heavy, slow, ponderous, rolling machines that would likely stop of their own accord if they were suddenly missing a driver. With any sudden, loud noise—even a blast from a diesel's air horn—Isaac would leap off his machine and dive for cover. It sounds funny to visualize, but it was not funny to Isaac.

Isaac suffered from an extremely severe case of post-traumatic stress disorder. Back then, it was called "shell shock" and it was the only recognized psychological stress disorder related to war. Unless they reacted as dramatically as Isaac, or withdrew completely like others, veterans suffering from what we know today as PTSD were simply ignored or ridiculed. Even shell shock had long been considered a coward's reaction. Today, we know it has nothing to do with courage or cowardice. Today, we know that military PTSD is a normal reaction to a traumatic situation. In addition, we know that just because a therapist's military clients do not dive for cover at loud noises does not mean they were not negatively affected by their service to our country. Research has shown that almost everyone who spends time in any of the services—combatants and noncombatants alike—suffer from military PTSD to a greater or lesser degree. How widespread the problem is among our warriors serving in Iraq and Afghanistan is now being acknowledged. Boot camp now includes preconditioning to help soldiers deal with the mental strain of the battlefield.

The VA is building a number of mental health facilities across the country, primarily to deal with the effects of PTSD and traumatic brain injury (another growing problem because the body armor that keeps our soldiers alive today also means they suffer more head injuries). The VA has acknowledged that, despite its best efforts, the number of deployed soldiers and returning vets with mental health issues is so vast that it cannot handle the workload. Its doctors aren't sufficiently trained, and assistance from therapists and psychologists in general practice must be sought. That is where you, the mental health professional, come in; do you feel trained to help our addicted heroes?

Nevertheless, nowhere in general psychology are therapists specifically trained to deal with the trauma of war and the pain of warriors. Civilian therapists understand that it is not the stress of a hard day at the office. It is also known that the symptoms of military PTSD are the same as nonmilitary PTSD, but, unless you have worked with veterans in the past, you also know there is a gap in your knowledge. That is where this book comes in.

How It Begins or the Root of the Problem and Possible Solution

Your client's military PTSD might be complicated by trauma he or she suffered before entering the service; this is called "complex military PTSD," and this condition can certainly increase the challenges facing our veterans.

On the other hand, your client may be one of those rare people who never suffered any type of grief, loss, pain, danger, or abuse in their pre-enlistment lives. If so, their PTSD is strictly related to their military service, which, in and of it, becomes an ongoing trauma from the first moment they step onto the boot camp bus and the door slams shut behind them. Immediately, they are yanked out of the life they knew and thrown into a surreal world that puts them at the mercy of some surly NCO (noncommissioned officer) who starts screaming because he or she is there to pick them up to start breaking them down. That is just in the first fifteen seconds of enlistment. The entire process of boot camp is to break the ego defenses of enlistees, brainwash them, and then rebuild the kill-on-command soldiers required for war. I believe strongly that we will have far less mental illness, addiction, suicide, and the heartbreak of a destroyed spirit if we counter-brainwash through the affirmation of forgiveness, atonement, and understanding how and why and what has happened to the soldier. We should provide integrated dual diagnosis treatment for our addicted wounded and traumatized heroes before they come home.

It does not get any better in boot camp. Enlistees are up early doing calisthenics, marching, double-timing, running the obstacle course, taking classes, disassembling and re-assembling their weapons, policing the barracks or the grounds, polishing their shoes, folding their clothes, and doing what they are told. Recruits are rewarded for good behavior and punished for bad. And if they should be so bold as to question an order, some NCO screams "Give me fifty" in their faces and keeps screaming until they count off fifty pushups to make it stop.

Every minute of every day is strictly controlled and carefully regulated; they do not know the daily schedule so they are at the mercy of their superior officers. They go to bed late and often hungry. The food in boot camp may be nutritious and it may even taste okay if you are lucky, but there is never enough time to eat it properly. Recruits soon cease to be their own person. Driven to the point of exhaustion in body, mind, and spirit, they become little more than cogs in the great machinery of war, to the exclusion of all else. Strict discipline, physical conditioning, automatic responses, and killing the enemy are what boot camp is all about. However, as distasteful and sometimes harmful as this is, there are valid reasons for it.

In the military, every job, down to shuffling papers and serving SOS, is dedicated to one thing: waging war. In addition, war is about death. War is about killing or being killed. Nothing is more basic, and very little is more traumatic. The goal of the military is to turn the raw recruit into a warrior who will obey orders without question, react without thinking, and most important, kill the enemy when the time comes.

With human beings being what they are, it difficult to turn a farm boy into a foot soldier, and basic training itself often leads to PTSD—again, a normal reaction to an abnormal situation, before they have even set foot on a battlefield. This presents a lot of problems for the military because all the brainwashing in the world can't control or even determine who will shoot to kill, who won't, or who will simply freeze "when the time comes."

As mentioned before, in a Civil War study, it was discovered that only about 10% of General Ulysses S. Grant's federal troops actually shot to kill in the Cold Harbor attack of 1864. The other soldiers either fired over the heads of the Confederate soldiers or joined the chains that were reloading and passing muskets to the shooters. Considering the confusing and traumatic nature of any civil war—cousin against cousin and brother against brother, you might expect the low shoot-to-kill numbers. However, in his book, *Reconciliation*

Road, J.D. Marshall examined the records of American soldiers who served from the Civil War through World War II and found that less than 20% of them actually fired their weapon at the enemy. There is little doubt that some of the low firing rate can be directly attributed to the ambivalence and avoidance that so often signals military PTSD.

Whether it comes from too much boot camp or too much war, the degree to which soldiers suffer from military PTSD is determined by the severity of their traumatic experience, how long it continued, and the response of those around them, especially senior officers who most often tell soldiers, "You volunteered—it's your job; it's what you're trained to do; it's you or the enemy; get your act together, soldier."

However, officers are not immune, and many suffer "survivor guilt." Author J. Glenn Gray, promoted to second lieutenant in World War II, wrote *The Warriors* in response to his own feelings of guilt and shame that still lingered fifteen years after his discharge.

Clearly, anyone who serves can suffer from military PTSD. A very important factor in determining the depth of the psychological trauma and addiction in the soldier is whether he or she killed another human. Just like the soldiers at Gettysburg, at some point the soldier had to choose whether or not to take another person's life. I repeat, more vets committed suicide after Vietnam than died in the Civil War! A moral dilemma faces every soldier on the battlefield because, before they joined the army, they were taught that killing a human being is immoral and reprehensible, not to mention against the law. No matter how well they have been trained, killing is never an easy decision. It can create ambivalence and self-hatred for following orders or for defying them (damned if you do, damned if you don't) at a time when they do not need to be confused. According to Gray, this combination can lead to extreme mental breakdown.

D.A. Grossman points out in his book, *On Killing*, that "the desire to kill after you look into the eyes of another human being and see them as human leads to the choice to not kill." That's why all the drilling and grooming in boot camp and A-school (Advanced Core Training) includes dehumanizing the enemy and indoctrinating the troops to hate them all—from Savages and Red Devils, Damned Yankees or Johnny Rebs, Krauts, Japs, Jerries, and Nips, Gooks, the Cong, the Commies, and the Rag Heads and Skirts.

It is important to realize that anti-enemy propaganda and indoctrination are not just the province of the military, nor are the consequences. The government waging the war promotes it to the public. Many, in fact, courageously responded to the latest clarion call to protect the nation in the wake of the 9/11 tragedies. We need to help our soldiers understand that the American public, unlike during the days of Vietnam when conscripted civilians were blamed for doing what they were forced to do, honors their service and strongly supports them as American fighting men and women. They need to know that support for our warriors has not wavered.

The therapists and healers among us who are dedicated to helping our veterans recover from their military PTSD have to allow history to judge the "right" and "wrong" of the wars in Iraq and Afghanistan. Our job is to help our warriors heal from the trauma of their service, to help them rebuild their lives outside the military, and to "wash out" the brainwashing that turned them into full-time warriors. To do that, we have to help them understand what happens psychologically when the military runs (or is it ruins?) their lives.

In order to transform them into the warriors/killers they needed to be, their previous lives had to be erased and new ones created. That is the job of the boot camp drill sergeant or company commander. The good ones are masters of "psychological orientation," the military euphemism for brainwashing. It is their job to traumatize recruits into being killers-on-command. Their motives are laudable—to protect our soldiers from the enemy so they can survive to carry out the mission, but their "psychological orientation" techniques can leave psychic scars on the toughest recruit. At some point in boot camp, for example, all enlistees realize that they are going to survive and will be warriors—trained killers. Self-confidence soars and a part of them begins to believe they will never feel victimized by anyone ever again.

Sadly, almost every belief with a magical "never" or "forever" attached to it is actually just another trance state: you have lost the ability to think logically and clearly. This is how I explain it to my clients: "Your military trance state begins on the boot camp bus, when that screaming NCO's threats and verbal attacks make you feel completely isolated, utterly helpless, and generally victimized—painful symptoms of PTSD, but absolutely necessary for a good brainwashing. Because of the abuse, you quickly develop hyper-vigilance, staying constantly alert to your environment, which is critical if you are to survive on a battlefield, but this is also another symptom of PTSD. These are just a few examples of how your military brainwashing also instills in you the basic building blocks of military PTSD."

The seven components of military brainwashing discussed below have been drawn from military training materials. When you read the following section, you'll understand why being isolated in boot camp for six or more weeks is necessary to program in the automatic reactions our warriors will need when they go into battle—the same reactions that later lead to the trance states inherent in and indicative of military PTSD. If you entered the military with other traumatic events in your past (complex military PTSD), you were already very "tranceable."

If you were mistreated as a child, you might hear a parent's voice in this list and quickly slip back into the trance state that helped you survive that early abuse. In addition to possible strong emotional reactions, you are likely to have a deep and intense learning experience as you consider the brainwashing you may have endured in your childhood and definitely endured in your military service. The goal of the therapist is to help these soldiers "de-trance," or "wash out" the brainwash. The military spent months preparing soldiers to go to war. A two-hour talk in a gym with two hundred other soldiers while turning back in their guns and uniforms, however, did not prepare them to come home. They are now different people, unfortunate heroes suffering from the trauma-related symptoms of military PTSD. Furthermore, their families, jobs (if they have jobs), and friends have all changed and moved on with their lives.

If you are a therapist, the following discussion will probably be painful for your clients. Nevertheless, it is also the first step on the road to recovery. What are their expectations now home from battle? Do they expect special treatment, a party, and gratitude for their service? How about basic respect? Sadly, this is not the experience of most soldiers. The following are the seven components of brainwashing.

The Seven Components of Brainwashing

- Obtain Power and Control
- Cut Off Outside Support and Validation
- Increase Sense of Powerlessness
- Manipulate Rewards and Punishments

- Shape Compliance through Small Steps
- Maintain a System of Logic
- Encourage Disorientation and Confusion

(Compiled by K. Evans from military psychological orientation materials.)

Obtain Power and Control

The first step in brainwashing is to obtain power and control over the victim. Because of their roles as father and mother, parents have "positional power" over their children, with the responsibility to keep them safe, love them, and teach them about safety and life. An over-controlling parent misuses this positional power until the children are not able to feel proficient at anything or develop healthy self-esteem or the skills necessary for emotional separation from the parent. The children develop a hostile dependency, where one part of the child hates being under such strict control while another part fears a scary world without the controller(s) directing his or her behavior. Drill sergeants everywhere have exactly the same power and control over their boot camp trainees.

Cut Off Outside Support and Validation

The second component of brainwashing is to cut off outside support and validation. In a domestic violence situation, the victimized spouse is not allowed to have relationships outside the abuser's circle of influence; it's as if the family is a closed unit, like a cult, which means there is less chance the victim will be believed. Abused children are not allowed to have friends. Girls who are victims of incest

usually are not allowed to date, join school teams, or participate in outside activities. A child who tells a family friend
or even her mother what "Daddy did," is likely to hear a
denouncement of that painful disclosure with an invalidat-
ing statement such as, "Your father wouldn't do that." Boot
camp is somewhat different, of course, because the "family
members" in that "closed unit" could easily validate your
client's experience by their own. Nevertheless, they cannot provide outside support and validation because they are
within the circle of abuse. Cutting off the outside world is
critical to any program of brainwashing; that is why boot
camp features weeks of complete control and complete isolation.

Increase the Sense of Powerlessness

Increasing the sense of powerlessness is the third step
in the process and it is often accomplished by the abuser(s)
wearing a mantle of authority: "I am your father/your drill
sergeant/your superior officer, and you will do as I say."

In Christian families, the biblical admonition to "submit"
is often used to support an abuser's "God-given authority" to
control children and wives, which creates in victims a lack
of faith in an ultimate power.

In boot camp, the same effect is produced when "God"
is mentioned only in connection with "damn" and "piece of
nothing" and/or your client is marched off to church every
Sunday where the chaplain (a superior officer) equates spirituality and patriotism with strict obedience to God and all
superior officers, who, incidentally, are the only ones who
seem to have the power to invoke God's name to damn a
worm like your client into fifty jumping jacks.

Manipulate Rewards and Punishment

The fourth component of brainwashing involves manipulating rewards and punishment. In the case of an abused child, he or she might receive "a special gift" upon compliance, but is also intermittently denied presents, love, or any support at all. This inconsistency is terribly confusing to a child and induces trance states regularly: the child cannot figure out the rules because they are always changing.

Boot camp rules are generally pretty rigid, and while the individual punishments are standard, "Give me twenty-five" of something, they are assigned at the whim of a drill sergeant, company commander, or any superior officer. This also means your client's punishment may be meted out to the entire company or squad, which often happens to those who question authority, in order to isolate them from their peers. On the other hand, boot camp awards go to a team, which manipulates the recruit further because it diminishes individual value and increases dependence on the closed unit. This leads to peer hostility and what is referred to as a "blanket party" (severe beating).

Shape Compliance through Small Steps

Component 5 involves shaping compliance through small steps, which means getting the individual to do one small thing then another. Remember the "rub my shoulders, sit on my lap" sequence in the earlier chapter? Boot camp teaches recruits to shout quickly, "Sir, yes, sir," then to make up their beds so a quarter will bounce, then to march in cadence, then to do calisthenics in perfect lines, then to—again, you get the picture. With each small step, they become more compliant. Moreover, if they should question their abuser about the "next step," they are blamed for having already complied by submitting earlier to the abuser's authority—"You never stopped me before, honey." "You took an oath to obey, soldier!" When it comes to PTSD, this is a golden nugget of self-blame, shame, and survivor guilt.

Maintain a System of Logic

Maintaining a system of logic is the sixth component of brainwashing. The perpetrator will offer a logical reason to follow instructions. A child might be told all children have sex with their parents. A battered spouse might be told again and again that it is his or her fault the abusive partner had to hit him or her; if the battered spouse didn't act in a certain way, the abusive partner would not be forced to slap, hit, or hurt the spouse. In boot camp, the logic is always the same—"It's the military way. Are you giving me trouble? Drop and give me fifty, instead."

Encourage Disorientation and Confusion

The seventh and final component of brainwashing is to encourage disorientation and confusion, and there is no better example than the military itself. Recruits and troops are kept exhausted, sleep-deprived, confused about what is going on, and are never told in advance what is going to happen because they don't have the "need to know." On top of that, the military is notorious for changing its mind without notice and often without logic. In basic training, when your client finally responded, "I'm just here to follow orders," the basic brainwashing was complete and he or she was well on the way to becoming a warrior.

It is important to note that boot camp is just the beginning of military brainwashing, but it sets the stage by preparing the warrior always to follow orders from anyone with higher rank and never to ask questions. The grooming continues in advanced training, particularly in doing things the Army, Navy, Air Force, or Marine way. The brainwashing continues at the next assignment, the next, and the next. Many military trauma survivors relate that deployment, when and where they were going, was always on a "need to know" basis, which meant they rarely knew what the next day might bring or even the next hour. To survive, they had to give themselves over to the brainwashing of the warrior culture. In the past the military gave soldiers two hours to be in formation and hop on a plane. They did not know the destination. It could be Iraq or a quick loop around Seattle and then back to McCord airbase. (Just a training exercise for readiness.)

Chapter 2 Questions

Brainwashing

Which components of brainwashing do you identify with the most from your life before the military?

1. People ***obtained power and control*** over me prior to my military experience when they:

2. I have felt ***cut off from outside support and validation*** prior to my military experience when:

3. I have felt an ***increased sense of*** powerlessness prior to my military experience when:

4. People have ***manipulated rewards and punishment*** prior to my military experience by:

5. People have ***shaped my compliance through small steps*** prior to my military experience by:

6. People ***maintained a system of logic*** that was not logical prior to my military experience by

7. People ***encouraged disorientation and confusion*** prior to my military experience by:

Building Soldiers <u>*Military Brainwashing*</u>

Now we want you to answer similar questions, but this time with your military experience in mind. Think about how the brainwashing in boot camp helped prepare you for war.

1. The use of ***power and control*** during my military experience helped prepare me for combat by:

2. ***Cutting off or reducing contact and support from non-military friends and family*** helped prepare me for combat because (e.g., When I had too much phone time with my wife, children, parents, siblings, or friends, I felt torn about where I should be and questioned if I had done the right thing.):

3. Feeling **small, helpless, and powerless** during my military training helped prepare me for combat because (e.g., I was taught to obey commands and not question a superior officer. When I needed to fall in, I naturally acted like a trained soldier.):

4. People **manipulated my rewards and punishment** during my military experience, which helped prepare me for combat because (e.g., I learned how to be a soldier and "kill or be killed."):

5. **Shaping my compliance through small steps** helped prepare me for combat because (e.g., If I had not been trained to automatically respond to threats, I would have been overwhelmed; an example of this is …):

6. **Maintaining a system of logic** during my military experience helped prepare me for combat because (e.g., I learned to react automatically under threat. It was my job to kill as a soldier. This helped me by …):

7. ***Encouraging disorientation and confusion*** during my military experience helped prepare me for combat because (e.g., It made it realistic. Once I was in Iraq, I was never going to be able to predict what was going to happen next, so I stayed prepared for anything and everything. When I think about this, I remember ...):

8. ***When I think about killing,*** I remember the following and feel:

Please answer these further questions about your military service.

9. ***If you did kill during the war,*** how many people? What are your memories and reflections on these events?

10. ***Do you have survivor guilt related to your deployment?*** Describe your symptoms of survivor guilt in relationship to killing or other issues:

You have just begun to UN-brainwash yourself! It is very important in the transition back to your family and a new war-free life that you are clear about which of the seven components of brainwashing most affected you. You need to let go of feeling broken now. You are no longer in danger; you are no longer a child or a recruit. You have grown mentally and emotionally as well as physically. You are a miracle and a strong soldier/survivor. You are "the Unfortunate Hero"; unfortunate because your name and your pain are not known or understood, nor can it ever be fully compensated for to you, your loved ones, or to the world.

Tips for Counselors

The issue of tranceability is very important. It is a strong and often deep form of hypnosis. As we continue to study the brain, both from neuropsychology and nerve damage from trauma, we find we only use 23% of our brain. Imagine if we doubled that? Trance work and the subtlety involved will help you and your client move through the pain and the process of recovery.

Chapter 3

Post Traumatic Stress Disorder further Defined

Post-traumatic stress disorder (PTSD) refers to a set of symptoms and problems that can develop after a traumatic event that is so intensely frightening, dangerous, and uncontrollable that it overwhelms our ability to cope and severely threatens our basic safety. PTSD has many causes. The trauma might involve surviving a war experience or being a victim of robbery or assault. The diagnostic statistical manual (DSMIV-R) is the psychologist's rulebook for diagnosing disorders. The following is from the DSMIV-R on PTSD:

309.81 Posttraumatic Stress Disorder 209 (APA)

A. The person has been exposed to a traumatic event in which both of the following were present:

(1) The person experienced, witnessed, or was confronted with an event or events that involved actual or threatened death or serious injury or a threat to the physical integrity of self or others.

(2) The person's response involved intense fear, helplessness, or horror. Note: In children, this may be expressed instead by disorganized or agitated behavior.

B. The traumatic event is persistently re-experienced in one (or more) of the following ways:

(1) Recurrent and intrusive distressing recollections of the event, including images, thoughts, or perceptions. Note: In young children, repetitive play may occur in which themes or aspects of the trauma are expressed.

(2) Recurrent distressing dreams of the event. Note: In children, there may be frightening dreams without recognizable content.

(3) Acting or feeling as if the traumatic event was recurring (includes a sense of reliving the experience, illusions, hallucinations, and dissociative flashback episodes, including those that occur on awakening or when intoxicated). Note: In young children, trauma-specific reenactment may occur.

The Four Senses: "Sight, Sound, Touch, and Taste"

All four of our senses can be affected by traumatic events. Perhaps you are aware of experiencing only one or two sensory reactions. However, these reaction(s) can be subtle and at times very confusing. When I say "sensory," I am referring to sight, taste, smell, feeling or touch, and hearing/sound. Perhaps you survived a fire where all possessions were lost or have that "burnt smell." You may have suffered burns yourself or had the *sight* of another being burned in the flames. A fire is often a shared trauma with many different triggers. To add to the trauma falling under the fire *smell*, what was it actually burning? Was it clothes and other items or people, such as in an A-bomb or airplane crash? Was there debris from the crash flying all around you? Were you trying to move to safety? Did you touch anything related to the crash that might leave you with a *touch* or *kinesthetic* memory of the event? Did you feel frozen or did you have to run to avoid getting hurt?

People *hear* numerous *sounds* connected to a fire following an airplane crash. Perhaps there was a lot of screaming and people yelling for help. Following a fire or disaster, there are crashing sounds and sirens from first responder emergency vehicles.

Taste is another sense that can be affected by the trauma. During the event, you may have tasted something that is triggered and reenacted. Maybe you or someone else was drinking alcohol during the event. Women who are raped by perpetrators who are drunk often are triggered by the taste of alcohol or another substance or food. They may be triggered by the taste of something similar and then they feel as if they tasted that substance again. In the case of a disaster such as a hurricane or flood, many things that you had to eat or drink may have made you sick.

The trauma may have been a single event. The symptoms may show up only during a particular situation and be limited in time.

Tom's Story

Tom suffered severe symptoms of PTSD. From the ages of six to fourteen, Tom was sexually abused by his uncle and physically abused by his stepfather. On one occasion, Tom tried to tell his mother about the sexual abuse. Her response was to call him a liar and say, "Go get the belt," to his stepfather, after which he underwent a beating so severe he had bleeding welts on his legs and back. Because of the intensity of his trauma and the age at which he experienced it, Tom had many symptoms of PTSD. Because the sexual abuse continued into Tom's teen years, he held a secret fear that he might be gay. In addition, even though he was a man, he hated men due to the physical abuse by his stepfather. Tom was heterosexual, but became very angry and confused about sexual identity and what it took to be a "real" man or strong woman.

When Tom drank, he got violent and homophobic and wanted to "beat up some queers." Tom had almost no memories of childhood; he had only vague surreal memories. Tom also suffered blackouts when he drank. Tom had no memories of the abuse (amnesia or dissociation). Tom always felt different from others—as if he never fit in with any group of people. Because of this, being part of a "group" of soldiers was one of the attractions to the military for Tom. Feeling as if you do not fit in is called "estrangement."

Tom had always felt that he was the target of others' criticism and that nothing he did was ever good enough. Even if he got praise from others, he felt as if they really did not mean it. He would feel patronized and talked down to, so he would not even try to accomplish things (victim-stance thinking and a pessimistic attitude). Tom felt anxious, depressed, and angry most of the time, and, although he pretended to feel things, he had few positive emotions (emotional numbing).

Even when he married, Tom did not feel sexually comfortable with his spouse. He could have sex only after having a few beers (trauma-related fears). He had few friends because he could never seem to let anyone get emotionally close to him (fear of abandonment, lack of trust, social isolation). Tom had a problem with his temper and sometimes exploded for trivial reasons (intense anger/rage). At other times, he would burst into a terrifying rage or panic and felt as if he wanted to run away for no apparent reason (flooding). Over time, Tom drank more and more and felt panicky at the thought of being unable to have a drink.

When Tom enlisted in the military, he started being triggered. Tom was deployed to Iraq. When on a convoy to sweep for bombs, Tom saw his best and only true friend blow up and evaporate right before his eyes. Tom shut down. He suffered complex chronic PTSD and addiction. He did not want to stop drinking, as he felt it numbed the pain. His drinking began to get out of control, and his PTSD got worse. Tom was medically discharged from the military.

Like Tom, you may have experienced one or all of these sensory triggers. These triggers may haunt you today in the form of a sensory flashback.

There are other types of chronic PTSD where poverty or starvation is the norm, such as in many third world countries. Children and adults who are physically or sexually abused can suffer from PTSD. Growing up with an alcoholic and/or mentally ill parent who said one thing and did another can result in PTSD. Another cause for PTSD may be an intense experience that caused feelings of extreme threat and insecurity. All of these experiences can cause PTSD effects later on in life.

The symptoms of PTSD fall into four clusters: avoidance, reenactments, victim-stance thinking, and shame.

Avoidance

- Amnesia (forgetting)
- Dissociation ("trancing out"—mentally going away to avoid a painful situation)
- Hyper-vigilance (being overly alert in scanning one's surroundings)
- Emotional numbing (trying to block feelings to avoid pain)
- Controlling behavior (trying to be in charge to regain a sense of power)
- Estrangement or social isolation

Reenactments

- Flashbacks of the traumatic event
- Nightmares of the event
- Flooding (being overwhelmed by feelings or memories)
- Overreacting to situations that resemble the event or reacting in self-defeating ways

Victim-Stance Thinking

- Distrust of others
- Feelings of abandonment
- Feelings of helplessness
- Great fear of change
- Blaming others for our own problems
- Unable to take responsibility for own healing process

Shame

- Feeling guilty
- Feeling as if we are bad or immoral
- Feeling as if we are crazy or sick
- Feeling as if we are unworthy or are "impostors"
- Feeling hopeless and lost on the recovery path

Three factors influence how severe the PTSD will be. The severity of the trauma is one factor. Examples of severe trauma include military combat, a catastrophic accident, domestic violence, or sexual abuse. The age at which the trauma occurs is another factor; the younger the person, the more severe the symptoms. The third factor is the degree of support that the victim receives from others during and after the trauma. This plays a big part in how well the person survives the experience. Being silenced, blamed, and shunned by others re-victimizes survivors. This can set up two interlinked themes: "I am not safe" and "No one will help." These survivors are often stuck in both the pain of what was done to them (the trauma) and the lack of support from others (abandonment).

These themes are the logic behind the trance. In counseling, we call this "trance logic." In the book, *Trances People Live* (Wolenskey, Guilford Press), the author describes dissociation as trance states. Furthermore, he discusses in detail each trance or dissociative state experienced by the survivor as being linear trance logic. By using what I call "parts therapy," you can get to the bottom of the barrel of trance states, which are strung together like links on a chain fence. When a link in the chain breaks, there is no longer a connected link of chains. To break or eliminate the dissociative trance link, we need to go through the chain link by link. We have to go through each link that links the trance belief to the next one to break up the dissociative chain that binds. I will attempt to simplify what can seem confusing; it is really quite logical.

When drinking to numb the pain is no longer a solution, it becomes another serious problem. A different example would be if you broke your leg and were in a cast. Your doctor and everyone else told you, "Do not try to walk on that cast, as you can hurt yourself." Perhaps you're a bit impatient and wanted a cool beverage, which was downstairs. In spite of all the warnings, you try to go downstairs alone. You do not want to ask for help, so down the stairs you go. By the time you hit the bottom, you have a broken arm, fractured wrist, and you have knocked out two teeth. When your spouse gets home, he or she gets very upset and tells you how stupid it was that you did such a thing. Your spouse asking, "How could you be so stupid?" really means, "I love you and I am worried about you." (Counseling and communication skills can help in the delivery of the message.) Now what is the result? Instead of just having one problem—a broken leg, you are a mess. PTSD and drinking is pretty much the same thing.

Chapter 4 will discuss the disease of addiction in more detail. I will mention some of the symptoms of addiction now so you can understand why you need to be clean to heal from PTSD. It requires a dual recovery program. Symptoms of addiction include *negative consequences* from the use of chemicals and *loss of control* from chemical use. Liver disease, heart disease, and lung cancer are examples of some of the physical problems that addicts may develop. They may experience social problems, such as being fired from a job, fighting with a spouse, or being charged with drunk driving. They may have tried to cut down or stop drinking but failed. Some common symptoms of addiction include:

- Lying about or denying chemical use, or minimizing problems caused by the use of alcohol and other drugs
- Preoccupation with use
- Failed efforts to cut back, quit, or follow personal rules such as drinking only with friends or drinking only wine or beer (loss of control)
- Increased frequency, increased amounts of use, or escalating problems as a result of drinking or using (progression)
- Needing more of the chemical to get the same effect (tolerance)
- Rapid intake
- Protecting the supply/hiding extra "just in case"
- Blackouts

- Family, work, and legal problems
- Withdrawal symptoms, such as the "shakes," restlessness, irritable feelings, sweating or mood swings

Synergism

Suffering from both PTSD and addiction is synergistic; that is, the combined impact on the addicted survivor is greater than the impact of each disease individually. In addition to the symptoms listed in the previous section, addicted survivors also experience strong, ongoing feelings of anxiety and depression. The false belief that only chemicals can relieve the pain develops. This belief may linger in recovery. This belief needs to be challenged and then changed by self-examination and by learning new ways to deal with the pain. Otherwise, the patient will continue to relapse into chemical use. Newly sober survivors may feel as though their PTSD symptoms are worsening. The chemicals may have helped temporarily block painful feelings, which are now returning. Addicted survivors often find themselves in a vicious cycle: their chemical use, once a solution, is now part of the problem. Their PTSD fuels their addiction, and their addiction fuels their PTSD.

Knowing the symptoms of your illness is an important step in the dual recovery process. It's a good idea to share your responses with a counselor, minister, or sponsor. I do not recommend a family member or someone who has been hurt by your drinking. They have their own bad feelings and need to share their feelings with someone else.

As discussed earlier, the symptoms of PTSD fall into four clusters: avoidance, reenactments, victim-stance thinking, and shame. I have left space where you can answer some questions regarding your own symptoms after reading this chapter. Remember, when learning something new or expressing your thoughts there are no wrong answers, just your answers. Some responses are more helpful than others. Whatever your experience is, it is unique. No one has the right to question or deny you your true feelings, thoughts, and memories. They are yours.

Abandonment

Another way one can experience symptoms of PTSD is after feeling abandoned. The experience of someone telling us he or she had our back in a fight or promised to "be there for us" and then did not show up can lead to feelings of abandonment. Feeling abandoned is a very common symptom of PTSD. In addition, it is a silent abuse by omission. It is not what the person did to you; it is what the person did not do for you. The fear of abandonment can be serious when it has not been treated in a therapeutic setting. It can cause all kinds of havoc. You might feel hurt and unloved by the smallest slight to you. This is like being picked last for basketball or not being invited to a party.

Perhaps as a child, you gave a party and no one came. While these may seem like insignificant issues, if you experienced these feelings young, this theme will play out your whole life. You may find that you are very clingy in a relationship and fight feelings of jealousy and insecurity. You may think your significant other does not love or care about you. In addition, you may address your feelings of abandonment by taking control and breaking off relationships that were perfectly happy because of your fear that the person might break up with you. You have a fear of commitment that keeps you from feeling close to other people.

Helplessness and Hopelessness

Feelings of helplessness and hopeless are common to someone who has survived trauma. Growing up in an alcoholic family can be an unpredictable experience. Your parent might act one way when sober and the opposite when drunk. In fact, a change in personality is one of the criteria used to diagnose alcoholism. There is a big difference between feeling helpless and powerless. When someone feels helpless, he or she often feels small and overwhelmed. The first step of the Alcoholics Anonymous program states, "We admit we are powerless over alcohol and our lives have become unmanageable." At first, you might think that helplessness and powerlessness are the same things. They are not. They are a paradox. They are the opposite of each other.

Many survivors try to be in control of things as a way to try to stay safe. We develop the peculiar belief, "If people would do what I told them to do, then everything would be just fine." Even if we are particularly intelligent or talented leaders, it forever holds true that people do not obey what we tell them to do! Don't they know that we are playing God and have only their best interests at heart? The truth is, they most likely see our attempt at playing God as, in fact, not very helpful. We get into a power and control struggle over the most ridiculous things. Alternatively, people ignore our well-intentioned advice and everything falls apart. We must realize that we are powerless to make others do what we want them to do. We all have free will. Running amuck and trying to control the uncontrollable can take us to our knees. When this happens, we have reached that decisive moment called powerlessness.

Helplessness is, in fact, very different. We give up without trying and play the victim. We look for other people to blame for our problems and worries. We attempt to not be accountable for our own behavior and behave as if we are helpless. There are many interesting stories about the idea of helplessness as being unhelpful. If you were starving and you came to me and said, "Give me some fish. I am starving," I might respond, "I will not give you fish this minute but I will spend two hours and show you how to catch your own fish so that you will never be hungry again." A person attached to helplessness and victim-stance thinking would call me selfish and go away hungry. However, the wise person would thank me for teaching him or her how to fish, thereby helping his or her family learned to fish so the person will not feel hungry or helpless again.

In the second scenario, the person is empowered, not helpless. The person who left feeling as if I were selfish was suffering from what we call "learned helplessness," and had learned to try to get other people to do what the person could do for him or herself. Staying helpless is a choice. All of us have had situations in our lives where, if it were not for the help from others, we might not have survived. However, choosing to be the victim and blaming others for your problems is a choice to be helpless. If, as a counselor, I try to do for my client instead of helping the client learn how to do things for him or herself, I have enabled the client to stay in a helpless victim-stance. I could say I am powerless over what choice my survivor client makes. The client has the right to be helpless; I am powerless over that choice. I do not particularly agree with the client's life choice, however; it is the client's life.

This takes us right into the issue of staying clean and sober. I will make strong recommendations that, if you follow, I believe will make you feel better than you can recall.

I hope that at least a part of you can see that safety and sobriety go hand and hand, and you will give this dual recovery program a chance; by doing so, you are giving yourself a chance.

You may have suffered things far beyond what I could ever imagine. I do not know the cause(s) of your PTSD—be it military, pre-military, or complex PTSD combined pre-military trauma. However, I can offer you this hope and even a promise that you will get better. Your flashbacks and nightmares can be reduced and your mood and sense of safety can be improved if you follow the recommendations for recovery.

In my job as a therapist, being an agent of change, I have met many people who came to me with a "fix me" attitude. They state they want to stop the pain and the outcome of the choices that they have made, but they do not want to have to change their choices.

In these situations, I am very direct and share that the only way I can help people find the personal and psychological safety they seek is if they change the individuals, places, and things that accompanied using drugs and alcohol and triggered unsafe situations to replay like an old broken record.

Great Fear of Change

Many alcoholics and survivors report that they "hate change," but it is not change itself that is difficult. It is the resistance to change that is the problem. Change will occur with or without your input. It is now one moment past me stating everyone changes. We just had a time change. I am still here; hopefully, you are, too.

Survivor Guilt

I have mentioned the symptom of survivor guilt. One example of survivor guilt is a child who is feeling guilty about being traumatized. The child did not understand that he or she was brainwashed and blamed him or herself. Even without the perpetrator of the trauma blaming the victim, it is a strange paradoxical control issue when we discuss who is to blame for the trauma. While you have been and will be told repeatedly that it is not your fault, there might be a part of you that blames yourself anyway. This same part of you thinks, "If only I would have done something differently, I would have not been a victim of trauma." If you were in a car wreck, you might think, "If only I had left the house earlier or gone another route," or, "I should not have been on my cell phone."

A friend of mine has a saying, "You can't hope for a better past." (Of course the childish part of me responds, "I can if I want to!" Brilliant, Dr. Katie; choose to feel guilty!) We may have survived trauma, but that does not mean that we have to live as a victim. You are not weak; you are a hero, even if you didn't get a Medal of Honor. You are living proof that you survived. You are here and able to help others survive through sharing your experience. If there is no logic to your pain, there is at least the opportunity you have to be a mentor and role model to yourself, others, and your family. Survivor guilt is a normal part of PTSD. Like all symptoms of this anxiety disorder, it serves a purpose.

Bob's Story

Bob had been in Iraq for over a year. He drank himself to oblivion whenever he had an opportunity. The last time, he ended up losing rank and had increased duty hours, as he got so drunk he missed his deployment due to being passed out on a stranger's couch. Bob did catch up with his platoon; however, the leader was not interested in Bob's excuse of blaming the alarm clock. Bob was very angry over this issue. He was very triggered and felt he was being punished unfairly and harshly, as the staff sergeant and he had gotten into it before over other "stupid stuff," as Bob explained.

Bob worked as a medic in a hospital located in a temporary interrogation camp. He did the intake and treated the wounded who passed through the door. Bob was a highly skilled medic. He had achieved rank and awards, but then lost them, as he lacked respect for his superior noncommissioned officer (NCO). His salutes were not quite what they needed to be. He smirked a lot and told jokes about this sergeant when he was not around.

One night Bob had to go on detail with a small group of soldiers led by the NCO Bob disliked. Sergeant Black needed a medic on this detail. Bob would not have been his first choice, as he thought Bob had an attitude problem. It was a dark night, without a moon or star in the sky. Bob and the others listened closely for enemy tanks or soldiers. Sergeant Black went first and was followed by two men, then Bob, and several other soldiers followed up the rear.

Sergeant Black had no more than spoken the command, "Watch your step," when the two men between himself and Bob, along with the two men behind Bob, stepped on trap bombs, which lit up like candles. Bob saw these men dissolve until all that was left was a boot, a left hand, and some shoes. It was pure luck that Sergeant Black had stepped over the trap bombs and Bob had dived ten feet after the first bomb, preventing his destruction like the two soldiers in front of him.

Bob was sick. He wretched in the bushes and collapsed as he saw the burning remains of the four bodies from his squad. The smell of death led Bob and Sergeant Black to vomit profusely. There were no troops in the area to call for backup. Bob, Sergeant Black, and the few men left tried to find the body parts of the burning remains. They got what they could and found all four of their dog tags. Bob was ordered to try to match body parts and separate one soldier from the other.

Sergeant Black followed protocol and took the ID tags and the remains to give to his superiors to forward to families. Bob was in shock. He could not speak. He went through and completed his job as if he were a zombie. Bob was dissociated, he felt numb. The questions that looped around in his head were, "Why them and not me? Why them and not Sergeant Black?"

Bob thought he would be able to sleep this off, but he could not sleep. The flash of the bomb, dismemberment of body parts, and smell of burning flesh kept Bob sick and wired. Bob slowly started to realize that he had survived a near-death experience that he would have been unlikely to have lived through. The question, "Why them and not me" spun in his head like a merry-go-round. They were better soldiers, they had kids at home, and he did not deserve to live when his friends did not. Bob was plagued with survivor guilt.

To make matters worse, Sergeant Black called Bob into the tent to talk the following day and demonstrated deep compassion and concern for those who had died, their families, and Bob. Bob could not believe that his sergeant, whom he had talked so badly about, could be so thoughtful and kind. This added to his guilt.

Yet, at one point in the talk with Sergeant Black, Bob blew up and yelled, "Maybe if you had your head out of your ass and paid attention to the convoy they would be alive. What's so special about you that you lived?" Bob then started sobbing, "What is so special about a drunk like me? I did not deserve to survive." Bob's head spun between anger, fear, and guilt so fast he stared at his boots. He could not sleep for three days.

What Bob didn't know is that Sergeant Black agreed with Bob at some level. He did not feel as if he had done his job. He had lost four men—all of whom had families. How many men had died on his watch as the sergeant, the one in charge? He should have known more. He was real army for fourteen years. He had shown Bob, of all people, that he was weak by throwing up in front of him and crying. The sergeant, like Bob, suffered survivor guilt.

The book *On Killing* discusses how many officers, who never actually saw combat, suffered from survivor guilt. The number of suicides of post World War II officers who "just sent men off to die" equals the number of those who led them to death in the field of combat. Survivor guilt can be very subtle, but is a critical key to healing for a self-blame survivor guilt trance state.

Ted's Story

A soldier I counseled, whom I will call Ted, was partying a lot and had dropped out of college. Ted lived with his parents at age twenty-four and worked at a fast-food diner. Ted's parents were not going to tolerate his lying around the house drunk, high, or hung over on the days he was not working. His parents got the father of a friend of Ted's to come over to the house and promote the idea of enlisting in the army. Four months later, Ted was in a Texas boot camp sweating profusely. Ted told me he realized immediately he had made a huge mistake.

Due to his low scores on the military entrance test, Ted had few career choices. It was off to combat in Iraq almost immediately. Ted begged by phone and letter to be discharged. He did everything he could, including a drunken suicide attempt to gain his parents' support. Ted's mother contacted a state senator who expedited Ted's medical discharge.

In spite of his desire to be out of the army, Ted suffered survivor guilt, feeling he had "weaseled his way out." To make matters worse, he drank more than a fifth of whiskey daily. It was his father who had talked him into going into the army, as his life was "going nowhere." Once home, Ted held deep resentment toward his father, whom he would frequently call during a blackout and yell at him for "trying to get him killed."

During our therapy, a day approached when Ted's anger at his father increased. The night before Father's Day, Ted got really drunk and told his father he was not going to be home to see him. Ted's mother came home from a last-minute shopping trip on Father's Day to find her husband dead. He had shot himself in the head for ruining his son's life. Ted's father also had survivor guilt—a secret he did not share.

In summary, as mentioned before, there are three factors that influence the severity of the PTSD. In Ted's story, the trauma affected many people.

1. The severity of the trauma is one factor. Examples of severe trauma include military combat, a catastrophic accident, domestic violence, or sexual abuse.
2. The age at which the trauma occurs is another factor: the younger the person, the more severe the symptoms.

3. The third factor is the degree of support that the victim receives from others during and after the trauma. This plays a big part in how well the person survives the experience. Being silenced, blamed, and shunned by others re-victimized survivors. This can set up two interlinked themes: "I am not safe" and "No one will help." To add to this dilemma survivors often blame themselves. These survivors are often stuck in both the pain of what happened to them (the trauma) and the lack of support from others (abandonment). This is coated with a sense of "I should have died instead of them" (survivor guilt).

Survivor reenactments, mentioned before, merit mentioning at least two more times. Hypnotic states developed from trauma and trance beliefs will suddenly appear unexpectedly. You may have done lots of therapy time in understanding reenactments, and then out of nowhere a survivor bursts into tears when they can't get the video camera to work. Consider the trigger of this reenactment as you answer the questions below.

Chapter 3 Questions

Recovery Activity: **Reenactments**

Flashbacks of the traumatic event(s). One or two memories repeat themselves in a flash memory or feeling as if I have been transported back in time. This occurs when I am triggered.

1. My triggers are:

2. My flashbacks are picture dissociations of:

3. I have had dreams like or similar to real events or nightmares of my military experiences where people are getting killed or blown up. Flooding (being overwhelmed by feelings or memories) occurs when something happens that leads me to feel like I am back in the military or when I feel small like a young child. I know sometimes these things are triggered by:

4. If I start to cry, I get more upset and feel really out of control. I tell myself, "Stop acting like a baby." I think the first time I was told by someone that crying was like being a big sissy or baby, either before I entered the military or after, was:

5. I have been overreacting to situations that resemble the event or reacting in self-defeating ways since I was a kid. I have always been sort of a hothead. Since being in the military, I find that at times, I have gotten so angry and full of rage that I have punched holes in the wall, yelled at my friends or family when I did not mean to, or lost control of my anger in other ways. The following are some examples of when I have lost control of my temper and I behaved in a way that was embarrassing or unsafe to others or myself:

6. Playing the victim refers to a state of mind or way of thinking where you feel like you were treated badly. You felt small and like a victim. You felt unable to be assertive and state your thoughts or feelings. On the other hand, you might have triggered and gotten very quiet or gotten very angry and said things like "That's not fair!" Think of times prior to the military or since your service where you felt like someone was putting you down or not respecting you and it was not fair. Describe a situation that comes to your mind:

7. Distrust of others is a common symptom of PTSD. There have been times in your life when you have felt like someone you admired and trusted betrayed you. The person did not listen to your side of things or may even have abandoned you. Describe an experience prior to the

military and one related to the military where your trust was violated:

8. You have survivor guilt, and feel like you could have done something different than you did or maybe wonder why you are even alive. Discuss your understanding about survivor guilt: I am beginning to see that drinking and using will make it difficult to get and stay sober because:

9. Does this apply to you? "This chapter made me think about the reality that my PTSD will not improve if I keep drinking and using, and I will not get and stay sober unless I work through my PTSD recovery at the same time as ceasing to drink and use. I will relapse on one or the other if I don't take it one day at a time and work on me. Recovery is a walk up a path; it is not a sprint to a finish line." Describe what is keeping you from accepting your poly recovery:

Tips for Counselors

It is critical that the simultaneous integrated recovery plan in this book be followed if they are going to be able to clean and serene. Anger and resentment are two emotions that must be worked through as part of grief and loss. There are many therapists who get triggered when treating individuals who are very angry. If you are not comfortable treating rage, it is in this part's therapy dissociation chapter that it will be recommended that you either get close supervision or bring in a co-counselor. Be sure that you do not fall into a trance state when doing trance work.

Chapter 4

The Disease of Addiction

Alcohol, in and of itself, is simply a beverage. This beverage has been served and celebrated in different forms going back to before the time of Christ. In most cultures, it has been developed for a variety of uses and in many different settings. The newcomer to the production and use of alcohol is the Native American. The Native American has no defense or "stop valve" in his or her brain. This stop valve in the brain is a biological ability to stop drinking after consuming a reasonable amount. Native Americans have a 90% rate of alcoholism if they choose to drink (Vaillant, 1995). Therefore, the early American-European settlers' "gift" of alcohol to their new Indian friends at Thanksgiving destroyed many lives and much of the Native American culture. When tested, Native Americans can show alcohol levels of 4.0, which in most cases would induce coma. In most states in the U.S., drunk driving laws for blood alcohol levels are .08. Blood alcohol levels over 4.0 are commonly found in the bloodstream of a Native American or alcoholic, or in some cases both (Jellnick, 1983). I would like to make it clear that I am not one who blames alcohol; it is not alcohol, in and of itself, that is the problem. It is who is drinking the alcohol that is of concern.

I used the analogy of Native Americans, as they are biologically different and unable to tolerate drinking like a nonalcoholic individual of another culture. PTSD alters the brain chemistry of the survivor. Nightmares and night sweats are examples of symptoms of altered brain chemistry.

If you pour alcohol on an altered brain with no stop valve, then disaster, destruction, and death can occur.

In the same light, drugs encompass everything from life-saving antibiotics to brain-killing street drugs such as meth-amphetamines, cocaine, ecstasy, and many other narcotics. I am not going to attempt to list each and every drug that is available legally or illegally today. I will discuss as a group the drugs that are mind and mood altering—drugs taken without the supervision of a physician and abused in order to feel "high." Marijuana is included in this category. Many people minimize the effect of "a little pot" just as they do "a beer" over the "hard stuff." A drink is a drug, and a drug is a drug.

Legal Problems

Obviously, if obtaining and using a drug is illegal, then drugs cause great destruction both in the individual and in our society. The demand for mood-altering illegal drugs makes the supply a lucrative business. Many deaths occur from the production and distribution of illegal drugs before the user ever actually partakes of the drug. Billions of dollars are made and spent in the attempt to stop drug profiteering. The individuals who supply drugs have a huge markup on their investment to grow or create illegal drugs. There are many deaths related to the competition of one drug lord with an-other to be the main supplier of cocaine or heroin. The United States government's attempt at stopping shipments of drugs coming into this country is a military operation in itself.

Current research shows that 80% of incarcerated indi-viduals were acting under the effect of drugs or committed crimes to obtain funds to purchase drugs. The average annual cost to incarcerate a person in this country is approximately

$30,000 annually. While in jail, obligations for child support and paying bills go unmet. Multiply this by the millions of individuals flooding our jails and penitentiaries. Multiply it by unpaid bills, child support, and taxes. It is obvious that we have a very expensive problem with these drug-related crimes. Drugs are often profitable to the dealer and destructive to the user.

Brain Damage

Battery acid, cleaning fluids, toxins, and various poisons are the meat and potatoes of cooking a batch of methamphetamines. Therefore, using a drug like meth is similar to snorting battery acid or gasoline. However, alcohol and hallucinogens have demonstrated the same destructive effects (Evans and Sullivan, 2001). The brain cell destruction and damage in the frontal cortex of the soldier's brain due to drug and alcohol abuse lead to a subgroup of addicts who already may have severe brain injuries. Both the addicts and the severely brain-injured soldier show no impulse control. A counselor running a recovery group for this type of subgroup may feel as if he or she is running a behavior management group for twenty grade-school-aged kids with attention deficit/hyperactivity disorder. Therefore, specialized integrated treatment ideas and materials are needed.

The particular parts of the brain affected by methamphetamine abuse may lead to impulsive sexual and violent behaviors and a loss of a higher consciousness and morality. It is difficult for many experts to agree if meth addicts will ever heal parts of their brain damaged by this toxic, popular, quickly addictive, and relatively inexpensive drug. Therefore, we need to have specialized integrated approaches for who enters our door (Evans and Sullivan, 2001).

In the last five years, there has been a huge increase of the use of "OC" (Oxycodone), which is synthetic opium manufactured for those needing acute pain relief. These pills are now being used and abused by teenagers, and a new heroin-type addiction has emerged. In fact, there are shortages in many pharmacies for these medications due to the high demand as well as an increase in robbery of pharmacies, hospitals, and veterinary clinics where these drugs are stolen and then sold at a huge profit. For the injured veteran with chronic pain, the risk for addiction is high. There may be no other options to treat intense chronic pain other than opiates. If this is the case, the PTSD treatment provider and the pain management provider need to work together to prevent overdose or abuse of needed medications for pain.

In the last decade, the evolving use of homemade drugs, such as methamphetamines, has been on the rise. The ingredients to make meth are easily procured. Without writing a recipe for what and how meth is produced, it is important to understand the damage that this one drug does to the individual who quickly becomes addicted. Meth, crack, ice, speed, and ecstasy all have similar byproducts. Most alarming is that the main ingredients include battery acid and other toxins. Brain function is destroyed, as is a person's ability to manage impulses, think rationally, and distinguish right from wrong.

Sadly, many soldiers have come home with head injuries from IED explosions or other types of cognitive injuries from car wrecks. I repeat that any use of a drug that damages a healthy brain is a bad idea. A traumatized brain does not and may not be able to recover if drugs are breaking down brain cells already depleted. Drinking and using drugs at all post-combat will interfere with your ability to benefit from your PTSD treatment.

Chemical dependency is a chronic, progressive, and potentially fatal disease. Some symptoms lead to negative consequences from the use of chemicals, such as incarceration noted above. For the purpose of this discussion, I am referring to alcohol as a drug. It is a legal drug for many adults, but a drug nonetheless. Negative symptoms include medical complications, including liver disease, heart disease, and kidney or lung cancer. In addition, brain cells are killed by the poison and overdosing of alcohol.

These brain cells are important to the overall functioning of your body. Your brain, like a computer, is in charge of a number of physiological performances in the human being. If you get a computer virus, you will not be able to utilize your computer and all of its special features. In fact, if you do not catch the illness in your computer, the virus can infect the entire functioning of your computer, ultimately causing it to crash.

I again want to point out that not all people who drink are alcoholics and not all drug users are addicts. At what point has the individual crossed over from a social user or abuser of alcohol and/or drugs to an addict or alcoholic? When the drug user finds him or herself labeled an "addict," he or she often suffers social problems because of chemical use. Already angry and resentful from PTSD, the addict is not very willing to accept saying farewell to that "old friend" alcohol. Perhaps over a period of time, non-drinking friends are simply "no longer fun." Personality changes from drinking or using drugs occur in all people. For the soldier, this personality change might lead to the surfacing of deep, longstanding resentments and hostilities. This could cause him or her to argue with superior officers or pick fights with other soldiers. The soldier could be deployed to Iraq or another area where alcohol is not readily available. The individual may go for months without even thinking of getting drunk or high. However, once on leave, the alcoholic more than makes up for this dry spell and may experience social problems. Perhaps he or she is argumentative. On the other hand, a shy person, after one or two drinks, is a teller of tall tales leading others to avoid the person's company due to dishonesty.

Alcohol and drug use is involved in 85% of domestic violence cases. Alcohol sedates the part of the brain than manages impulse control. A verbal argument may break out between spouses or with a child, which then escalates to domestic violence, leading to possible criminal charges and even restraining orders.

While military personnel are aware of the rules and regulations about drinking and driving, these rules may be disregarded. DUI charges will be the result of too much alcohol and too little good judgment. After being charged with drunk driving, military personnel can lose rank. They may be finding or face incarceration due to inappropriate behavior. Extra duty and restriction can also be part of the punishment and/or consequences. Alcohol and drug use may cause a soldier to fail to show up for roll call or fail to show at all ("what is the point" attitude). An abuser may have tried to cut down or stop. Ultimately, the person most likely loses control.

Some people try to stop drinking hard liquor but continue to drink beer. However (since beer is alcohol), inevitably some common symptoms of alcohol abuse will progress into the disease of addiction, the disease of denial.

Lying about chemical use or denying/minimizing problems caused by the use of alcohol and other drugs is the foundation for this disease of denial.

Symptoms of Alcoholism

- Preoccupation with use
- Failed efforts to cut back, quit, or follow personal rules, such as drinking only with friends or drinking only wine or beer (loss of control)
- Increasing frequency, amounts of use, or escalating problems as a result of drinking or using (progression)
- Needing more of the chemical to get the same effect (tolerance)
- Rapid intake
- Protecting the supply/hiding extra "just in case"
- Blackouts
- Family, work, and legal problems
- Withdrawal symptoms, such as the "shakes," restlessness, irritable feelings, or mood swings
- Using to avoid withdrawal

HALT and SPORTS

PTSD and Drug and Alcohol Use Synergism: 1 + 1+ 1 = 3

Suffering from military-induced PTSD and addiction is **synergistic**; that is, the combined impact on the addicted survivor is greater than the impact of each disease individually. In addition to the symptoms listed above, addicted survivors also experience strong, ongoing feelings of anxiety and depression. So, 1 (PTSD) + 2 (PTSD & addiction) = 3.

Due to the denial associated with addiction/alcoholism, it is best to hold off on requiring the fragile, distrustful survivor with huge control issues to label him or herself as an alcoholic. However, I ask that a "no use" contract be signed during the course of integrated dual diagnosis treatment. I define alcoholism as what causes problems is a problem. If the survivor cannot keep the contract, then the survivor demonstrates that he or she is powerless over the use of alcohol. I work on building trust and repeat the fact that alcohol use is unsafe behavior.

The attempt to medicate the pain of flashbacks and nightmares is huge. Antidepressants and other non-addictive psychiatric medications do not work the same way as alcohol and take much longer to kick in for full effect. The pace of healing PTSD symptoms is slowed, if not stopped, if drinking is continued. I want to be clear that drinking or ongoing continued use of drugs is different from a serious attempt to stay clean and relapsing. The model for trauma and addiction recovery discussed in the following chapters works with relapsing. That is not to say that relapse is permissible but that it happens. We want the addicted survivor to stay engaged in treatment and not end up drunk or dead.

It has been my experience that discussing abstinence as a safety treatment issue weeds the true addicts out from the abusers. Ongoing relapse offers a lesson from a mistake. Refusal to try to stop drinking requires a more restricted environment for safety and detox. Denial is so paramount to this disease, yet, once there is acceptance, there is a true epiphany. The adage "I am sick getting well, not bad getting good" releases a great deal of shame that overwhelms addicted survivors.

Using alcohol or other drugs can lead to the triggering of PTSD symptoms, including reenactment of terrible violent events when deployed. It is important that initial stabilization of PTSD and addiction work is done to develop some skills for psychological safety. A knowing relapse trigger is important.

In addiction treatment, "HALT" is a short check for pre-relapse behaviors. Ask yourself, am I: H (Hungry), A (Angry), L (Lonely), and/or T (Tired)? If the answer to any of these questions is yes, you need to halt, take a deep breath, and use your tools for recovery. We will discuss specific safety skills in the following chapter.

Let me use the example of basic training where soldiers are taught how to assemble and shoot a gun. "SPORTS" is a shortcut recall to the step-by-step process of a weapon stoppage. S (slap: the magazine of the gun), P (pull: charging handle), O (observe: observe chamber), R (release: release charging handle), T (tap: tap, forward assist), and S (shoot: bang, take cover!). Each of these steps is repeatedly practiced. A good soldier could master performing the SPORTS checklist in two to five seconds.

Consider for a moment the point I am making with dual diagnosis, PTSD, and drug use. Would you take a gun, now ready to fire, and pour a bottle of Jack Daniels on it, light a match, and drop the flame on the alcohol-covered weapon? Doing so would most likely lead to a devastating explosion, killing or maiming you and those around you. When you are a trained soldier, you are like that gun. You are trained to fire on command. If alcohol goes down your throat, leading you to amplify your pain, rage, confusion, paranoia, you become the weapon of self-destruction. Yes, you felt hopeless and at times helpless to do anything about your double-trouble of PTSD and addiction. Anyone with PTSD cannot find the way home to sanity and safety when using and abusing alcohol. This is true whether you are an alcoholic or not.

Alcohol deadens the frontal lobe—the judgment and impulse control of the brain. If you put this part of your brain to sleep, then you are no longer in control of your behavior. An intoxicated person with PTSD is a danger to him or herself and those nearby. The PTSD survivor does not need to be an addict or alcoholic to discover that alcohol and fire cause an explosion in your life. You are functioning out of the reptilian core of your brain. Fight, food, and fornicate are the basic human caveman motives. Drunken cavemen under these circumstances would have tried to pick a fight with a dinosaur—not too smart. Yet, when intoxicated, everyone finds they do things with people or to people that are not of their true nature or value system.

Take the example of Mark, a Gulf War veteran. Mark tried psychotherapy once or twice to try to help him with flashbacks of the war, but found that he only felt worse when he talked about it. A counselor suggested to Mark that he was an alcoholic, pointing out, for example, that he drank a six-pack a night and that his wife was threatening to divorce him if he didn't stop drinking so much. Bothered by these two problems, yet too overwhelmed to do anything different, Mark continued to drink. Over a period of six months, his mood worsened and he drank even more. Overwhelmed by the memories of his combat experience, Mark tried on several occasions to kill himself while under the influence of alcohol. Mark thought that he could never sleep or turn off the "war channel" without alcohol. What he did not realize was that, by drinking during his PTSD therapy, he was making himself worse. Alcohol ignited the smoldering rage inside him. Then Mark found a counselor who was trained in PTSD and alcohol and drug counseling. He quickly found ways to stop painful triggers and reenactments and found that the VA had psychiatrists who are trained in using non-addictive medications that helped him sleep at night as well as reduce his depression.

All survivors are at high risk for addiction. We often turn to chemicals to "medicate" our pain and begin to believe that only chemicals can relieve it. This belief may linger in recovery. It needs to be challenged and then changed, by self-examination and by learning new ways to deal with the pain. Otherwise, we relapse into chemical use.

Newly sober survivors may feel as though their PTSD symptoms are worsening. The drinking or drugging may have helped block painful feelings (or so they thought) that are now returning. Addicted survivors often find themselves in a vicious circle: their chemical use, once a solution, is now part of the problem. Their PTSD fuels their addiction, and their addiction fuels their PTSD. That is why best practice treatment for coexisting PTSD and addiction requires an integrated treatment approach.

It is a good idea to share your responses to this exercise (and to the rest of the exercises in this workbook) with your counselor, a knowledgeable sober person you trust, such as a friend from your PTSD counseling group, a sober buddy, a twelve-step sponsor, or a minister. Sharing is likely to help you keep a balanced, realistic view and it will give you a source of support and validation.

Instead of the SPORTS drill reminder of weapon stoppage, lighten your load with SPORTS in recovery: S (see), P (people), O (overcoming problems), R (recovering), T (thriving), and S (soldier survivors).

The next chapter will discuss the map back home. Dr. Michael Sullivan and I developed a five-stage model for integrated recovery from PTSD and addiction. Over the last fifteen years, I have adapted this model to address issues related specifically to military post deployment trauma. Much has been studied over the past twenty-five years validating that addiction is a disease. If you doubt that the client believes that when his or her PTSD improves, social drinking will be an option, give a reminder of the AA saying, "Once you are a pickle, you can no longer be a cucumber."

__Chapter 4 Questions__

Recovery Activity: **Identifying Symptoms of My Dual Diseases**

1. Chemicals helped me block the following unpleasant feelings:

2. My chemical use has caused me several problems, including the following:

3. Three things that showed me my chemical use got out of control:

    a.

    b.

    c.

Symptoms of Alcoholism

4. I believe that I might be an alcoholic and/or addict because I exhibit these symptoms of the disease (please check the symptom(s) below that applies to you):
    o   Preoccupation with use
    o   Failed efforts to cut back, quit, or developing personal rules to try to control my drinking, such as drinking only with friends or drinking only wine or beer (loss of control)
    o   Increasing frequency, amounts of use, or escalating problems as a result of drinking or using (progression)
    o   Needing more of the chemical to get the same effect (tolerance)
    o   Rapid intake, drinking games
    o   Protecting the supply/hiding extra "just in case"
    o   Blackouts
    o   Family, work, and legal problems
    o   Withdrawal symptoms, such as the "shakes," restlessness, irritable feelings, or mood swings
    o   Using to avoid withdrawal

5. Other people failed to support, protect, or help me deal with my trauma. They blame me because I was drunk when:

6. I feel intense shame about drinking too much because my behavior gets out of control when I (give examples):

7. Two things I learned in this chapter are:

   a.

   b.

8. Two things that give me some hope that things can get better are:

   a.

   b.

As you finish this exercise, congratulate yourself. You are now beginning to turn things around. You are not alone! Read on to discover some solutions to support your recovery from PTSD and addiction.

Chapter 5

A Five-Stage Model for Sober Soldier Survivors

Recovery is a process, not an event. That is why we, as addicted survivors, talk about ourselves as being "in recovery" and not "recovered."

The recovery model for PTSD and addiction has five stages: *crisis*, *building*, *education*, *integration*, and *maintenance*. Certain tasks must be accomplished in each stage before advancing to the next. If these tasks and goals are achieved, transition to the next stage of recovery goes smoothly. If the tasks and goals are not met, going to the next stage does not go smoothly. We may get overwhelmed, feel hopeless, or even experience a relapse. A relapse might be taking drugs, which are not prescribed to you, getting high, or getting drunk.

Sometimes we start to give up and relapse, but then stop ourselves; we have a drink or drug, then stop. We realize this is not what we want to be doing. This is known as a lapse. You did not have a full relapse; instead, you fell down, got up, and got right back on track. Should you lapse or relapse, call your sponsor and/or go to a meeting and admit you have slipped and get the drugs and alcohol far away from you. If the substance is in your home, get rid of it. If you have gone to a slippery place, leave. I do not recommend that you keep alcohol in your home, as temptation is too high. One bad moment can lead to an impulsive relapse.

I will also comment here about keeping paraphernalia like marijuana pipes as souvenirs of "back in the day." When you get clean and sober, you need to get rid of all alcohol, drugs, and paraphernalia you have. You may want to have a ceremony where you and a sober friend break or bury that special pipe as a symbol of breaking off old things related to drug use. If you should slip up, simply step back a stage in the recovery model and see if you missed something. Perhaps there is that one secret you are keeping. Remember, you are only as sick as your secrets. Write about it or share it with a sober friend, counselor, or sponsor. It is important to remember we are progressing in recovery.

(A copy of the Twelve Steps of Alcoholics Anonymous can be found in the appendix section of this book. When the terms "meetings," "sponsors," or "the step" are used, these are references to Alcoholics Anonymous.)

We typically revisit each stage, but each time at a more advanced level in an upward spiral. There is often pressure in the military to make your fellow soldiers look good. Inside the walls of a twelve-step meeting, you and your soldier friends will find a sense of safety and solidarity as you share honestly about your addiction.

Many people are under the mistaken belief that heroin detox will kill you and alcohol detox is like a bad case of the flu. It is important to know that the opposite is true. It is alcohol, benzodiazepams, and other "downers" that are fatal if abruptly stopped without a medically supervised protocol.

Heroin does not kill you from detox, although many narcotic addicts feel like they are going to die due to the severe flu-like symptoms. Afghanistan is known for its production of opium. Like Afghanistan, Asia is an opium capital, and many Vietnamese and American soldiers were strung out on heroin or opium derivatives. The Far East and Middle East make a great deal of money from drug trade; oil is not the only local commodity sought.

The Middle East is considered "dry" due to religious beliefs, not just because of the hot and arid desert environment. Alcohol is less available in the Middle East, but can be found. A big drunken "welcome home" party is a dangerous beginning to numbing the pain of war with the oblivion of alcohol and many other drugs not mentioned above.

The most important fact I am trying to make is that many soldiers evaluated for intake may be drinking enough alcohol to avoid withdrawal symptoms. Alcoholics are not good historians concerning how much they drink, even if they could remember. If possible, a five-day short-term medically managed detox, using Librium or other cross-tolerant drugs, can ease the discomfort of hallucinations, sweats, seizures, and potential death from cold turkey alcohol withdrawal.

Any drug that our body is dependent upon will lead to some type of detox experience, even if mild. Those of us working with marijuana addicts are well aware of the mood swings, impatient behavior, preoccupation, and craving that accompanies THC withdrawal. When a person is detoxing off any drug, the world and its time and space are distorted. It feels to the addict like time has stopped. Hearing the saying "one day at a time" seems and feels like one day is too long to wait. Maybe the addict is feeling out of control or even suicidal. It is important in this crisis stage to do safety checking for no self-harm (Brown and Miller 1993).

It is never too soon to begin relapse prevention work. Picture a survivor in a relapse mode where the alcoholic feels at risk due to relapse from drug cravings. Now couple this with being overwhelmed by flashbacks of seeing body parts, bomb explosions, or the memory of shooting the first person who would have harmed you or others had you not followed your military training and eliminated the threat. This is an overwhelming crisis stage experience. Many survivors may want to keep these thoughts to themselves; encourage them to talk. If you notice a fellow soldier looking bad, get help. This is not like or being a tattletale; it is like calling 911. You could be saving a life. The worst thing that can happen is that the soldier on the fence of relapse acts angry towards you. Remember addiction is a disease. If you saw a person get hit by a truck and fall on the ground with blood streaming from their body, would you worry about making them mad? Of course not. In the addict/alcoholic life, the truck is alcohol or other drugs; the injury is the relapse.

Talking to other soldiers may cause some survivors to feel like whiners, and they may feel weak or less of a soldier (Kennedy and Kelley, 2008). Remember for yourself and others, it takes courage to step up and tell the truth even when you do not feel like it. Most likely you would have stuffed all the feelings and not talked to anyone at all. This is what leads to suicide, relapse, and having a psychotic break. Sharing with your spouse on a call from home that two of your friends were blown up in front of you today would traumatize your spouse and escalate the situation. Your spouse, the one person you used to share everything with, is now on a "need to know" basis. You are a soldier. That is the mindset you need to survive. This mindset will increase your own ambivalence about being in the military and being a soldier when your spouse calls and cries about your children missing you and wanting you home. The uncertainties of your situation and the confusion about what is the right thing to do can lead you to feel like you are in an emotional sandstorm. You may have double-trouble and have a flashback or reenactment of your past trauma. Suddenly you freak, freeze, or fight. Your brain starts to race. "What should I do?" All of the signs of the reenactment of feeling trapped are present. You feel spaced out and confused—signs of trance states.

Example Trigger: Spouse calls crying or yelling, "Come home now!"
Crisis Stage Intervention #1: Sensory counting

Use sensory counting to quietly and quickly stop the flashback or reenactment. We were born with five senses: sight, touch, smell, sound, and taste. Counting three of the five senses can work just as well, depending on your trigger. Count at least three of the five sensory experiences and do at least three rounds of three.

Let us use Mike's story to demonstrate sensory counting.

When Mike was a young child, his parents raged at him when they were drunk, which was a good deal of the time. It did not matter whether or not Mike had done anything wrong for him to suffer the sudden attacks of rage. What seemed to trigger the raging was how much Mike's father had drunk. In Mike's family, he was used as a "live answering machine." The scenario would go like this: Mike would innocently be playing with Legos. The phone would ring, and his mother, who had far exceeded her "happy hour" drinking, yelled at Mike, "Answer the phone! If it is your damn father, tell him not to bother coming home."

Mike felt sick to his stomach as he approached the ringing telephone. Dizzy and afraid, he knew this was not going to end well.

Mike answered the phone, "Hello."

Mike's father responded in a loud, slurred voice, "What the hell is going on there? Get your mom on the phone!"

Mike froze. There was really no right answer that he could give his loud, drunken father that would deescalate the problem.

Mike knew passing on his mom's message was a very bad idea. The next sound was Mike's father raging even louder.

"What's the matter with you? Are you retarded or deaf? Can't you answer a simple question?"

Mike noticed it was hard to breathe. His face felt hot, and he smelled his mother's whisky breath still on the phone. Mike felt trapped so he dropped the phone on the ground without hanging up and ran out the door.

As he was running, he could hear his mother yelling, "Where the hell do you think you are going?"

Mike hid in his "secret hiding place" all night until his dad was heading to work the following morning. Mike knew that his dad would come home that night and "beat his ass." His only hope and prayer was that his dad had been in a blackout when drinking and had forgotten what happened.

Now back to the here and now. Mike's wife called and was angry with Mike. She was raging at him on the phone, "I need you here! You need to tell the Army to kiss off and send you home where I need you!"

Mike felt sick, dizzy, his face was hot, and he felt afraid and wanted to run away. All military personnel know that leaving AWOL is desertion; military prison would be the next stop. At the moment, prison did not seem like an unsafe choice. Mike and everyone else on the planet but his wife knew you cannot just tell your CEO to "kiss off" and pack up and request a seat on the next flight out. That next flight would be to Ft. Leavenworth, Kansas!

Mike felt like a helpless child. Sometimes he would not even remember his wife had called (dissociation). He could not magically go back home and make his family happy nor could he make the bombs stop or end the war or the heightening sense of arousal in which he now found himself. He lapsed into a trauma-induced trance state.

This normal response happens to those who have been in Mike's shoes. It is important to remember, you are not alone! Listen to the sound of your own breathing. Breathe slowly and deeply. Use sensory counting. What is one thing you see? What is one thing you hear? What is one thing that you can touch or feel with your body? Now do this exercise again. What are two things that you see in the room with you right now? What are two things that you hear right now? What are two things that you can touch or feel with your body? Repeat again, now asking yourself what are three things that you see in the room? What are three things you hear in the safe room that you are in at this moment? What are three things that you can touch or feel with your body? Three sets of three—see, hear, and touch.

This works great to bring you out of a flashback or trance state and back to the moment in which you truly are. If, however, you are not in a safe place, do not use this method of trance busting. Get somewhere safe first! Remember, your spouse is still on the phone wanting a response. You do not have to fight or freeze; after sensory counting, you are out of your trance. Say, "Goodbye. I love you," and hang up the phone. You do not have to hang up or stomp on the cell phone. This crisis intervention technique saves a lot of money replacing cell phones!

Mike used to hide at the bottom of a bottle of scotch. The first two drinks he consumed helped him start to calm down. By his fifth drink, he was becoming loud and obnoxious. He looked at his watch, and he was already thirty minutes late getting home.

His friend Tom said, "Hey, if I had your wife I would not go home at all!" Both men laughed drunkenly.

Nevertheless, Mike started to feel that sick feeling. He was short of breath and had a hot face. He threw up after a quick sprint to the front door of the bar. His wife would not let him in the house. She called his first sergeant. Mike was on his way to recovery. Hung over and embarrassed, he felt like he was on the road to hell. He did not realize he had taken his first step on his path to recovery.

Crisis Stage Intervention #2: Breathing

Notice that you are breathing. Slow your breathing down and breathe more deeply. Suck in your navel as you breathe from your stomach. If you are triggered with anxiety, you are breathing from your chest and it is shallow and rapid breathing. That keeps you anxious. Your brain and body need oxygen; slow your breathing down.

Crisis Stage Intervention #3: Having a safe place

Now imagine that you have a safe place to go in your mind. If no place is safe, then create a place that is safer than most places. Perhaps it is somewhere you have been before. On the other hand, maybe it is a picture of a place you have seen where you wish to be. You can now imagine that you are in this safe place. You can even begin to tell yourself that this too shall pass. When you have established good breathing and have stopped hyperventilating, take a big breath and congratulate yourself for getting out of a tough situation. All that matters in this moment is that you find a way to feel safe and grounded. By using these skills from the crisis and building stage of dual recovery and not getting drunk or loaded, you will no longer have to run and hide.

If you become overwhelmed with the craving to drink or use, the three-times-three technique of sensory counting can work for preventing relapse for you as well. Safety is always what to find first.

You may need to find a safe person to talk to about traumatic memories or intense cravings. If no one is available, write about it. It is a bad idea to get loaded over it or, alternatively, to go get drunk after it. This is a bad idea, as it not only might take you out of recovery completely or lead you to do something that could harm yourself or others, but it also messes up your brain chemistry.

When you experience a traumatic event, you end up imprinting the memory chemically. If you have access to the Internet, go to www.amenclinics.com. You will find scans of brains on drugs and/or alcohol and scans of brains where trauma has been endured. These scans show how such behavior or trauma affects chemicals that your brain needs to survive. When your brain is sucked dry and washed away by drugs and alcohol, you risk suffering permanent brain damage. Relapsing when you are a soldier survivor, as with other sober people, can result in a number of negative outcomes. The obvious outcome is that you lose your sobriety and feel defeated or worse, yet you will imprint the bad memory and have twice the mountain to climb later.

Maybe you are in an unhealthy or abusive relationship. You need to begin to address this to get and stay safe and sober.

You may fear that the program won't work for you. It works if you work it. There is no problem that you have that getting drunk is going to make better.

A crisis is what brings most of us to treatment. Sometimes the crisis is deliberate and therapeutic, such as a family- or work-sponsored intervention (in which family and friends lovingly confront us with the stressful impact of our chemical use or other negative actions so that we will stop drinking or using other drugs and seek help).

More often, the crisis is unplanned, frightening, and confusing. Possibly our marriage has ended, or maybe we face charges for drunk driving or assault. Perhaps we receive an angry phone call from our mother who has never admitted responsibility for failing to protect us from abuse. In some cases, the custody and the safety of our children have led us to a new bottom.

In a crisis, both physical and emotional safety is a concern. Our physical safety could be endangered, for instance, during withdrawal from chemicals, which can be life-threatening if not managed by medical personnel. We can also get ourselves into dangerous situations when intoxicated, such as fighting in bars, driving drunk, or thinking about overdosing. Our living situation may even be unsafe or unhealthy. If a person who lives with us is drinking, using drugs, or threatening to harm us, we must do what we can to get safe.

Being emotionally safe means taking steps to protect ourselves from others—especially if those we live with ridicule, taunt, threaten, or humiliate us. Our spouses may criticize us, call us names, or threaten to beat us if we are not compliant. We need to learn how to set boundaries and limits for ourselves and find a safer living environment.

Our goal in this crisis stage of recovery is preventing imminent serious physical and emotional harm. By completing Step One of the Twelve Steps of Alcoholics Anonymous (admitting we are powerless over alcohol and that our lives have become unmanageable), we can increase our insight into our chemical use and other areas of our lives. Keep in mind that powerlessness does not mean helplessness. Paradoxically, Step One can help us feel empowered to change unsafe behaviors or situations.

The following list describes some strategies for staying safe:

- Briefly checking into a hospital for safety or for detoxification
- Calling the local AA hotline or another hotline
- Go online to www.alcoholicsanonymous.com where you can find AA meetings on the Internet all over the world twenty-four hours a day
- Making a contract for safety (a commitment to a friend, sponsor, or therapist not to attempt suicide or to use chemicals)
- Attending twelve-step meetings
- Reading the Big Book and other AA-approved literature
- Taking non-addictive medication such as antidepressants if prescribed by a medical doctor who is aware of the addiction
- Reviewing the copy of the twelve steps in Chapter 8

Building—Stage Learning new Skills

The goal of the building stage of recovery is to become better at protecting and nurturing oneself. Such skills will make our lives safer (and more pleasant).

Some of us never had the chance to learn these skills. Moreover, some of us already have many of these skills, but we may have difficulty using them when we are very upset.

Many communication skills books measure the feelings and expression of anger on a point system. The number 1 rates a passive response or no anger to a previous trigger for anger. The number 10 would be at the highest most intense feeling of rage. That would put assertiveness between a 4 and 6.

Assertiveness: An important skill to work on is assertiveness. Assertiveness is the ability to firmly stand up for yourself without being aggressive or running away.

Assertiveness is truly its own reward. Once I learned how to be politely assertive, I found that my requests were met. This skill can be used in a situation as simple as ordering a steak in a restaurant. In the past when I got an uncooked steak, I would either not eat it, try to get someone at the table to trade plates, or quietly ask the waiter for help. Sometimes this worked, but, if the waiter was too busy, I might be ignored. Now, I assertively but respectfully let the waiter know that my steak needs to be put back on the grill; it is not what I ordered. I am polite, but firm.

Setting boundaries is another skill that helps with recovery and life. This means learning how to set boundaries and learning to say no. We need to take every opportunity to practice setting boundaries, both externally and internally. An external boundary is a limit we set in response to someone or something outside ourselves, such as telling a critical parent not to speak to us in an unkind manner. Instead of experiencing endless feelings of shame that arise when we feel someone is unkind to us on the phone, we can ask that the person not call us if he or she cannot behave in an appropriate manner. I realize this may sound scary. You cannot worry about how the other person feels or thinks about you or about pleasing the person if you are going to set a boundary. No one can say no but you. If you want to stay sober and safe, you will have to say, "Please do not call me again," to a person drunk or high, who was an old partying friend or a dealer.

An internal boundary is saying no to all forms of harmful self-talk—for example, shaming ourselves and imagining that we will always be unloved if we do or do not do this or that. Any thought you have with a "should" on it is most likely not helpful. Be kind to yourself.

One day I was at the eye doctor getting my glasses. My health insurance carrier said they covered 100% (or so they stated). Then, when checking in at the doctor, I was eavesdropping on the call between my insurance company and the receptionist. Suddenly they no longer covered this eye doctor. I would have rated the receptionist's assertiveness at a 2, maybe a 3. So I asked to speak to the insurance company representative. I said, "How can we make this a win/win situation for both of us?" The receptionist and doctor were impressed. I was not pleased because I did not win. I did get the eye appointment covered at a better rate. In the past I might have gone to an 8 or even a 9 and stormed out of the building. By using the sensory counting discussed in this chapter, I at least did not look like a lunatic. I later got the bill in the mail. The insurance did pay half, which is sort of win/win. I give myself a 6 rating on the anger scale. My husband, who was the somewhat objective observer, sweetly commented that since I was shaking he thought it was closer to a 7.9. (Boy, does he know me well!)

Other types of assertiveness include expressing our concerns to others directly, asking for help, and negotiating compromises. Asking an objective observer how it looked to him or her can teach you reflective listening skills.

We can further protect and nurture ourselves by completing Steps Two and Three of Alcoholics Anonymous. Step Two can enhance our sense of faith and hope, our sense that someone "out there" can help us and things are better today than yesterday. Step Three can help us learn to let go of the obsessive need to control everything, by turning over control to our higher power, thus ridding ourselves of useless fear and worry.

Working these two steps when you are an addicted soldier survivor can be very difficult. On the one hand, you might not believe that there is a God. How could a God allow the horrible things to occur that you have seen? On the other hand, you might have been raised believing and trusting God. Maybe you feel angry or abandoned by God. I often point out to survivors that they seem to be angry with a God that they deny exists. That is indeed a confusing situation—a dilemma that must be addressed if a solid faith is going to be reestablished with a higher power.

Some additional sobriety skills you may find helpful in recovery include:

- Practicing relaxation and mediation
- Creating a schedule that includes a balance of work activities and fun
- Sober activities, health and fitness, and time with family and friends
- Learning to express feelings by sharing in twelve-step meetings
- Practicing complimenting ourselves
- Participating in a recovery group with other solider survivors who are sober

Education Stage

In the education stage of recovery, the goal is to transform our sense of self from that of victim to survivor and ultimately a thriver. We deepen our understanding of the complexity of having developed PTSD and addictions when what we wanted was to serve our country. Reading about our military trauma and recovery is helpful. Recognizing the impact our trauma and addiction has had on our lives and learning what we can do to promote our own recovery is essential. We want to begin to feel that we are truly survivors filled with courage, not victims filled with shame. We ultimately become thrivers when we can see the promises in the Big Book come alive in our lives.

We are not responsible for the cause of our diseases, but we are responsible for finding solutions to manage them. If we understand their processes and can name our symptoms and their roots, we can become stronger as we overcome our trauma and learn that we no longer have to be victims or even survivors. We are thrivers! As one solider said, "I used to feel like a wounded dog. Now I feel like an unfortunate hero." (A special thank you to Brandon, as that statement helped motivate me to write what you are reading now.)

Reading books, listening to tapes, and attending workshops and lectures about addiction and PTSD are important tactics in the education stage. By attending and participating actively in meetings where other survivors discuss their recovery, we can celebrate survivors' strengths and learn helpful ways to express and cope with pain from other sober soldier survivors.

During this stage of recovery, we need to try to remember that our own recovery comes first. If we are triggered and begin to feel overwhelmed when doing education work, we need to stop and use our safety skills until we feel safe and sober again. We also need to beware of taking on too much of the pain of others, trying to "rescue" others, or starting romances with other survivors when we are early in recovery and possibly vulnerable to exploitation or at least diversion from our recovery. Many of us are nurturers and natural caretakers of others. However, we oftentimes neglect our own self-care. This must change.

Integration Stage

The goal of the integration stage is to be able to safely and fully experience, in the here and now, all of our actions, thoughts, feelings, bodily sensations, and memories. We want to feel comfortable when alone and with other people. Gradually, day-by-day, we walk through the stages of recovery. We learn to laugh and not take ourselves so seriously.

Trauma occurred because we could not successfully fight back or escape the shock that overwhelmed us. In addition, the trauma worsened because we could not stop to process our grief and loss and get validation and support from others. Typically, we coped in the only other way left (other than death): we "disconnected" from others and ourselves as a final solution to an intolerable situation. Alcohol and other drugs helped us unplug from life.

Dissociation refers to our mentally checking out. When we dissociate, we usually develop at least three parts to handle the trauma: Dissociation often works so well that it becomes habitual. We may come to rely on it to help us cope with many aspects of our lives. Chemicals reinforce this habit; they too disconnect us from others and ourselves and block true awareness.

Unfortunately, this survival strategy has its cost. Apart from the original trauma, we have experienced many additional shocks and losses because of our PTSD and addiction. Perhaps we have run away from home or quit school early to escape an abuser. Perhaps we have lost jobs or marriages because of our addiction. We have lost not only our innocence and faith but also, when we are in recovery, our best "friend" in the world: alcohol and drugs. We have a great deal of unfinished business from the past stored in our wounded part, which keeps our energy for growth unavailable. Our protector part continues to be overly controlling, hostile, critical, or "nice." Our nurturing part either remains underdeveloped or is short-circuited. Moreover, our parts do not work well together because they are dissociated.

We continue our dual recovery by striving to rediscover, reclaim, and reconnect with all of our "parts" so that we can feel like complete human beings. By gradually allowing ourselves to become aware of all our thoughts, actions, and feelings and by working through them and accepting them, we can put it all together and become integrated. We also need to grieve our losses and let go of the past by working through our anger and depression and by reflecting on and accepting the impact the losses have had on our lives.

Work on integration can proceed in a number of ways. Continued work on Step Four can be helpful; an accurate inventory of ourselves can enhance our self-esteem. Some other ways to work on integration issues include the following:

- Keeping a daily journal to reflect on our experiences
- Writing poetry, painting pictures, or using other artistic means to express feelings
- Using our skills like sensory counting and deep breathing to stop a flashback or anxiety attack
- Going to meetings
- Working with others who are in need

As always, we need to keep safe. Integration work can cause pain, and we can go only as far and fast as we can tolerate. Take one day at a time.

The help of a professional who understands dual recovery from PTSD and addiction can be invaluable in this stage. He or she will notice any dissociation and can help with such tools as hypnotherapy. Working with a professional is particularly important if you plan to confront an abuser or if you have severe symptoms of dissociation (hallucinatory-type flashbacks, large memory gaps in both the remote and recent past that are not due to blackout, and flooding that incapacitates us). It is important to feel safe with this professional. Make sure he or she is trained in survivor and addiction therapies.

Maintenance Stage

The final stage of recovery is the maintenance stage. Since we are "recovering" and not "recovered," we need to keep our recovery program active and ongoing. We want to keep an ever vigilant eye toward preventing a relapse in either of our illnesses. We also want to continue to grow more fully as human beings. Working Steps Ten through Twelve and continuing to participate in twelve-step meetings and psychotherapy sessions are ways to do this. Service work, whether through being a sponsor in a twelve-step program or lobbying for laws to help other survivors, can also be an important part of our work in this stage. Having learned new solutions for old problems and having transformed our sense of the past, we are free to move forward into the future, one day at a time. The promises of recovery are now coming true.

No matter what your stage of recovery, it is a good idea to complete the next exercise, "My Safety Plan." If you begin to feel unsafe for any reasons at any time, put this plan into action. Safety is the foundation for a dual recovery program for PTSD and addiction.

Later exercises address issues relevant to the building, education, and integration stages. This workbook does not include exercises for the crisis stage, other than the safety plan. Nevertheless, remember, if you are in crisis, seek help immediately.

In addition, there are not any specific exercises for the maintenance stage. Instead, a section on relapse prevention has been included.

Chapter 5 Questions

Recovery Activity: **My Safety Plan**

1. I feel unsafe (or I want to drink or use) when:

2. When I feel unsafe, some safe places I could go include:

3. Some people I feel are safe and supportive for my dual recovery include (write down their names and phone numbers here):

4. When I feel unsafe, I can do these three things to stay safe:

   A.

   B.

   C.

5. When I feel like I want to drink or use drugs, I can do these three things to stay sober and safe:

A.

B.

C.

If you begin to feel unsafe for any reason, put this plan into effect.

Recovery Activity: **Building My Safety Skills**

If we have strong skills to protect and nurture ourselves, we can stay safe. The following exercise can help those of us in the building stage to develop these skills.

1. Read a book or listen to an audiotape on assertiveness and on relaxation. Write down the names of the books or tapes you chose; then list the two most important things you learned from them.

A.

B.

2. Describe a time when you told someone you disagreed with his or her opinion. How and when did you do this? How did you feel? Why was it okay for you to do so?

3. Think of a time you said no to someone, and explain how it felt. Why was it okay to do so?

4. Give an example of a time someone asked you a question you were not comfortable answering, and you stated clearly that you would rather not respond:

5. Name a boundary you set lately that you felt good about:

6. Name boundaries that you need to set, but have not done so. What fear has made you unable to set this boundary? How might you feel less fearful?

7. Why is it important to let go of whether the other person will still like you before you set a boundary?

8. Think of a time you have been angry recently but did not express your anger. Describe the situation. Why didn't you express how you felt? What could you do about this? Was the situation safe for you to discuss your anger or resentment?

9. List two healthy ways to express anger.

    A.

    B.

10. List two helpful ways to release stress and relax.

    A.

    B.

11. List two ways to manage feelings of depression.

    A.

    B.

12. Think of a time you asked someone you felt safe with to help you with something. How did you feel? How might you do this again?

13. It is important to make time for yourself on a regular basis. What can you do for yourself this week? In future weeks? How can you have fun, relax, and take yourself less seriously?

14. Think of something you have wanted to do for a long time. Imagine that your higher power is making this happen for you. Develop a systematic plan to accomplish this goal, and ask for guidance to get around obstacles that might get in the way.

15. Identify three of your strengths.

A.

B.

C.

16. List three things you do that you feel good about.

A.

B.

C.

Recovery Activity: **Education Stage—Emerging from Victim to Survivor**

This exercise is for readers working on the education stage.

1. I have learned that I am not a victim. I am a survivor because:

   A.

   B.

2. An example of victim-stance thinking is:

3. I know I give my power away when:

4. The three most important elements of my recovery program for my addiction and trauma issues are:

   A.

B.

C.

5. I am learning more about my recovery from PTSD and addiction by doing these things:

   A.

   B.

6. I have learned that some of my PTSD symptoms include the following:

7. Three reasons why staying clean and sober helps me in my PTSD recovery program are:

   A.

   B.

   C.

8. Attending a support or therapy group regularly is important for me because:

9. What I find most helpful about my support or therapy group is:

10. Sometimes I have found it difficult to tell my story to others because:

11. Some things that I could do to make telling my story easier include:

12. Thinking of myself as a survivor in recovery, not a victim, helps me by:

Recovery Activity: **Self-Evaluation**

The next exercise will help you determine your stage of recovery. Together with the information in the preceding sections, this exercise will suggest issues you might address on your own or with the help of friends or professionals.

In the following section, circle the number of each item that applies to you. Make a comment indicating if it relates to now, how you used to feel, or when you feel triggered. In the model for recovery, you may have built excellent strength but have some triggers that feel overwhelming. Look at the model of recovery stage by stage. It is like a constant spiral. Stepping back to pick up a new skill is enriching your recovery. It is not a sign of failure or relapse.

Crisis Stage

1. I regularly feel as if my life is out of control and unmanageable.

2. I sometimes feel that death is the only relief I may ever know from my pain.

3. The only way I know to stop the pain is to get drunk or high.

4. I often feel that the program doesn't work for me.

5. I often think about the "good old days" when I used to drink and use drugs.

6. I often question whether I am an addict and/or alcoholic.

7. Hurting others or myself somehow helps my emotional pain.

8. I often question whether I have PTSD.

9. I am currently in a living situation or relationship that poses an immediate danger to my health or safety.

10. I am in a living situation or relationship in which I face regular and severe criticism, ridicule, threats, and harassment.

Building Stage

1. I am usually comfortable calling my sponsor or other supportive person when I am having a problem.

2. I think asking for help is a sign of strength.

3. For the most part, I can tell someone no, if I do not want to do something.

4. I generally stand up for myself.

5. When someone criticizes me, I no longer feel overwhelmed with hurt.

6. I usually find that I can express my needs and opinions without blowing up.

7. Even when I have many things to do, I usually know where to start and what I need to do to get them done.

8. I can usually tell someone directly when he or she has hurt my feelings or made me mad.

9. I rarely engage in sexual activity when I do not want to (even if it means hurting my partner's feelings).

10. For the most part, I find that I can get organized and accomplish what I set out to do.

11. I no longer go into rages where I pick fights or hit walls.

12. I seldom find myself reacting impulsively or overreacting to situations and people.

13. I know how to manage the flooding of my emotions so I can generally handle painful feelings.

14. For the most part, I can put worries out of my head after I have done what I can.

15. I can use skills like sensory counting to managing disassociation and flashbacks.

Education Stage

1. I am generally familiar with the symptoms of both PTSD and addiction, and I understand how they apply to me.

2. I have a good sense of what I need to do to recover from my dual diseases.

3. I have spent some time reading about and/or listening to knowledgeable people talk about the causes and remedies of my addiction and PTSD.

4. I can discuss what my dual recovery issues are and what I need to do to work on them.

5. I have some idea why certain things are triggers for me.

6. I have connected with others who have the same issues that I have.

7. I have shared my story with others and am becoming more comfortable doing this.

8. I generally accept those things I am responsible for and can hold others accountable for what they are responsible for.

9. I can admit my mistakes and apologize to others without feeling ashamed.

10. I know that I am not alone and that I am one of many other solider survivors in recovery.

11. I know that I no longer have to be a victim or victimize others; I am a survivor.

12. I know my strengths and usually feel good about myself.

Integration Stage

1. I usually have no trouble staying in the here and now and I do not "lose" periods.

2. I know what I am feeling and why I am feeling that way.

3. I know how to manage my triggers.

4. For the most part, I have eliminated self-defeating behavior from my life.

5. My memories of the past are not vague or particularly overwhelming.

6. Generally, I know who I am and what I believe.

7. I have grieved my losses and have come to accept them.

8. I have stopped feeling stuck on any of my recovery issues.

9. I know my "parts," and they usually work well together.

10. I find that I am usually at peace with myself when I am
    _____.

Maintenance Stage

1. I know that I am recovering and will always need to work a program.

2. I routinely take the time for reflection to see how I am doing in my recovery and to spot potential problems.

3. I continue to find new ways and new situations in which to grow.

4. I still work at deepening my spiritual program.

5. I am trying to carry the message, even if in just a small way.

6. I read from one of my books that have positive spiritual energy:

7. I ask myself, "What step am I working right now?" Then I journal about my trigger and the step serves as a solution to the problem.

8. I ask myself, "What Step am I working right now?" Then I journal about my trigger and the Step serves as a solution to the problem.
   I remember the (Four Agreements,) or other good living principles that help me get out of myself, and stop worrying about things I cannot control. I stop my all-

or-nothing black-and-white thinking. Which are listed in the back of this book, are a thinking style that has caused me pain and trouble,

If you circled any of the items in the crisis section, get help now from friends and/or professionals. If you could not agree with two or more items in any of the other stages, you need to work on that stage.

Recovery Activity: Integration Stage

"Learning about the Different Parts of Me" and the "Grief and Loss Inventory" are two exercises for readers working on the Integration Stage. The first exercise will help us get to know our different parts better.

The second exercise will help us identify where we are in our grief process. Remember that a trained therapist is needed to help you with successful integration stage recovery work.

Recovery Activity: Maintenance Stage

1. I read from my Big Book.

2. I go to twelve-step meetings regularly.

3. I work the twelve steps of recovery.

4. I talk to my sponsor.

5. I have a strong relationship with my higher power.

6. I carry the message to other dual-diagnosed people whenever possible.

7. I remember slogans such as, "This too shall pass."

8. I have a circle of friends who are in recovery.

9. I try to work my own program and not control others.

10. I try to take my medications and work my trauma/addiction recovery program one day at a time.

Counselor Tips

Discuss medications with your client alone and in-group. Make a distinction between the drugs from the partying days and taking drugs as medication. The latter are now keeping your client feeling stable and are part of the recovery tool kit. They are drugs designed to help the PTSD, not run to old memories and to work my trauma. You might want to assist the soldier in making a list of helpful medications taken and unhelpful. Review this weekly in individual counseling or in a group therapy setting.

Chapter 6

Preventing and Managing Relapse

Relapse means the return of harmful feelings, thoughts, and behavior that were characteristic of us before beginning recovery. "Relapse is a process, not an event," to quote Terrence Gorsky, a well-known expert in treating, writing, and training counselors about relapse. You can find references to his extensive work at the end of this book. We can relapse in our recovery from chemical dependency by taking mood-altering chemicals, thus endangering our safety and sobriety. We can relapse in our recovery by smoking and engaging in many other unhelpful behaviors, some of which are triggered due to an emotional relapse, such as stress, anger, or abandonment. Oddly, since nicotine is a stimulant, it always seems a bit strange that soldiers who smoke increase PTSD by engaging in unsafe behavior, such as allowing suicidal thinking or returning to an abusive relationship.

However, we can also experience the feeling forms of relapse to PTSD. We can find that our old protector part once again kicks into full gear, causing us to be very critical of others and ourselves or to be very controlling, acting better than others in recovery. Alternatively, we may find that we are once again trying to do everything by ourselves, not asking anyone for help.

When working with dually diagnosed clients who are suffering great cravings to drink, there are solutions. See a physician familiar with alcoholics; have the doctor do some liver testing.

This function testing can tell if you are a candidate for Antabuse. Antabuse is a perception medication that can fight overwhelming cravings or preoccupation thinking when they are reminded, "I will be very sick if I drink today. I guess I will have to wait a couple of days." By then the "one day at a time" philosophy has kicked in, preventing relapse. Sometimes a judge will order a chronic drunk driver to take Antabuse, often ordering that it be monitored by a pharmacist to be sure it was taken. If someone drinks after taking Antabuse, an allergic reaction occurs. The person will feel flushed, nauseated, and throw up. It can be quite serious and the alcoholic needs treatment at an emergency room.

I recommend this only for the individual who wants sobriety but suffers many cravings. This is a last resort taken by a recovering alcoholic who wants to stay sober. They take it themselves before cravings start. The desire to drink is over when reminded, "I took Antabuse."

Remember that addiction is a disease of denial. It lies to you and lies to others. As discussed earlier, head injuries sustained from the war or from a car wreck leave us with a confusing sort of denial.

I was in a car wreck ten years ago, when I was fifteen years sober. I was T-boned in my SUV by a compact car. I was banged up, but did not seem too bad until the next day when my brain began to swell. I developed vestibular, or balance, disorder from inner ear fluid. This caused dizziness, unstable walking, then, bam—I would drop suddenly and hit the ground. This led to three more concussions in the next two years. I was very confused and had terrible short-term memory. I was forgetful, and I was going through a legal hearing with car insurance. My business associate would phone me and yell at me. Any intense emotion was very loud and overwhelming. I had word-finding problems and would get lost driving my car to the local store.

I had a long fall from success to feeling useless. I babbled so much my friends could not follow what I was trying to say. I fell into a terrible depression common to people who have both PTSD and head injuries. The PTSD from the car wreck continues if triggered by a driver who passes on the right or pulls out of nowhere.

I knew I needed help. It took a team that included a neurologist, speech therapist, psychiatrist (for medication), surgeon, physical therapist, and psychotherapist. Vestibular disorders affect hearing, sight, and balance. It took over five years for me to be stable enough to feel safe and function. I had a faith relapse. Once I pulled out of the depression, I found my previous relationship with my higher power led me down a curvy path, taking me here where I could at least share the subtle symptoms of my injuries. I set up a system: never make a serious decision after 7:00 p.m., and end conversations that are hostile and unkind. I kept notes so my memory could have assistance.

I will share parts of my personal story with you, to offer my experience and strength in hopes of reminding us both that we are sick getting well, not bad getting good. Recovery is a process not an event. I will always be in recovery from addiction as long as I do not drink or use/abuse drugs. I will never be completely recovered. Due to the changes it causes in my biology, I cannot be a social drinker. Eventually I would lose control of my social drinking and negative consequences would return. How long it will take for you and how well you recover depends on following your treatment plan, staying clean and sober, and being patient.

This is also true about the head injury I got when I was hit by a car. At first I could hardly speak. Over time I returned to a stable, better me. Because I was seen as a high-achieving person with lots of survival resources, no one offered to help except a couple of lifelong friends and my adolescent children. Those with closed head injuries look the same as they did before, so others do not realize that the hard drive (the brain) needs some new software. Every day I did what I could to get up, get dressed, and take newcomers and those I sponsored to a recovery meeting. Ever so slowly, day-by-day, I got better and found myself—a different new self. My faith returned directly in relationship to how much energy I put into helping others. I never really wanted to drink, but it felt like my higher power had gone on vacation. In retrospect it was myself who had focused so much on my problems that I forgot solutions were already waiting for me to arrive.

Terrence Gorsky, a friend and an international expert in relapse prevention, has written about cognitive behavioral interventions and relapse prevention. His work is easy to find on the Internet. He writes about how helpful positive affirmative statements are in your recovery program. He distinguishes a "lapse" (brief fall from recovery with or without actually drinking) from a "relapse" (when you cannot pull out of the lapse and you do old behaviors, see using friends, go where people are using or drinking as if it were fun "back in the day"). In a relapse, you can find you are drinking and using again. How long the relapse last depends on you and your willingness to get back on program.

Making a distinction between a lapse and a relapse is helpful. We have a lapse when we briefly slip back into our old behavior but then quickly pull ourselves out of it and restart our recovery program. We have a relapse when we continue to engage in old patterns and do not use the new skills and support we have developed in our program to get ourselves back on track.

Relapse can be one or all parts of your co-occurring disorders. You need to remember that there is nothing that the old drunk raging inside you is going to make better.

I believe nothing happens in God's world by mistake. I got remarried to a retired soldier and saw the variance of PTSD from the military than other sources. My point here is I had a lapse in faith. God sent in the military to restore my faith. You or I can have a bad day, a lapse in our program. That does not mean we will drink or use drugs if we get reentered again by using a recovery tool. I am grateful to be "me" again, and hope my story and this book help you.

Making a distinction between a lapse and a relapse is helpful. We have a *lapse* when we briefly slip back into our old behavior but then quickly pull ourselves out of it and restart our recovery program. We have a *relapse* when we continue to engage in old patterns *and* do not use the new skills and support we have developed in our program to get ourselves back on track.

Many of our veterans returning home have physical pain that is real from polytrauma. Having had their hands and legs blown off gives both acute and chronic pain where narcotics may be used. This is a very controversial issue in the addiction treatment field. There is no reason that our veterans should have to suffer chronic physical pain with PTSD and recovery. Working with a psychiatrist who is also an addictionologist is often very helpful. These specialists are often found at the VA. Recovery entails knowing ourselves well. We need to know not only which of our old behaviors are most likely to recur but also what issues to be aware of that might trigger a lapse or relapse.

The two main factors triggering a lapse to chemical use are (a) positive expectations of use and (b) managing negative emotions. *Positive expectation of use* refers to the thinking that life was or will be more enjoyable when drinking or using. People who glamorize the good old days, or who think that since they have worked on their PTSD, they can safely return to drinking and using, run the risk of relapse.

The antidote is to learn to enjoy life in recovery. Remember that we have so much to celebrate. We are blessed. We have been spared fatal and progressive diseases. Only 39% of people who recover from addiction are sober ten years later, depending on what research is studied. What many newly recovering addicts fear is how will they be able to have fun in life, without using. "What will I do if not drugs to feel good or have fun in sobriety?" Terrified of boredom, the addict and alcoholic prefer the drama and trauma of a drug-addicted life. The alcoholic part of their brain thinks that there is nothing to do if not partying.

Many alcoholics and addicts have delayed emotional development compared to those individuals who learned how to overcome the nervousness of asking someone out or a date or even calling them on the phone. Do you remember the awkwardness of that first middle school dance? The girls stood on one side the room and the boys stood on the other or went to the gym to shoot hoops.

In one treatment center I ran, I asked a good AA music band to donate a couple of hours. We had a recovery dance for the teens in our treatment center. I felt at first as if I age regressed to about twelve. I had with butterflies in my stomach. Finally, a few of us staff members dragged some kids out on the floor, and fun was had by most.

Intimacy and relationship skills can also be delayed by using; in our chapter on families, we will discuss this more in length.

Managing Negative Emotions

Managing negative emotions has been an excuse to drink or use. You now have learned other skills that are more helpful than numbing out the feelings. In the past, you may have been using chemicals to self-medicate unpleasant feelings. If we start to believe that we cannot take the pain without a drink or drug, we have fallen into a mode of thinking that increases the risk of a relapse. A good recovery program for PTSD and addiction can help us better deal with painful feelings through the social support found in twelve-step meetings and through learning skills to safely cope with feelings. (Gorsky, 1982).

Regardless of how well we work our program, we are likely to encounter situations and times when our recovery is at risk. The risk of relapse is part of recovery from any chronic illness, and we are in recovery from two illnesses. When a lapse occurs and a full-blown relapse is imminent (notice we say "when," not "if"), we need to have a relapse management plan to keep the lapse from becoming a relapse.

Remember, we are sick getting well, not bad getting good. We deserve to be treated with love and kindness by others and by ourselves. We are heroes. You need to honor yourself and what you did for our country. If friends, family members, or even our counselors get angry at us when we relapse, we have the right and responsibility to set a boundary with them and tell them that we deserve to be treated with love and kindness. If we are beating ourselves up, then we need to tell that not-so-helpful critical part of ourselves to back off. We need to ask, *Is it helpful to be so hard on myself?* We need to learn how to have love, compassion, and forgiveness for ourselves, just as our higher power has for us.

The following exercise will help you identify triggers for relapse and pinpoint some things that you can do to prevent a relapse.

Recovery Activity: **My Relapse Prevention Plan**

I know that drinking or using is not an option for me today. The negative consequences of drinking or using include:

1. I sometimes think of hurting myself when:

2. I drink and use to escape from:

3. Some situations that trigger my desire to drink or use include:

4. A person who I think of as a hero is:

5. A time when I think I acted like a hero was:

6. I feel confused and overwhelmed when:

7. I was told I helped others when:

8. Three fun activities I can do to replace drinking or using or hurting myself are:

   a. _____

   b. _____

   c. _____

9. Three people I can call when I feel low or am thinking about relapse are:

   _____ phone number: _____

   _____ phone number: _____

   _____ phone number: _____

Recovery Activity: **Recovering from Relapse**

1. I relapsed because I:

2. The excuse I used was:

3. Before I relapsed, I could have prevented it by:

4. I did not honor my need for safety when I thought:

Chapter 7

Vicarious Trauma

Empathic burnout and vicarious trauma are terms used to describe what happens when the therapist begins to get symptoms of PTSD from listening to the PTSD experienced by the soldiers and family members they counsel and serve. It is not unusual for therapists to become overwhelmed by the soldiers' experiences. It is a side effect of treating our wounded warriors or any wounded person. Being a helper too long with too many people without a break for support can cause burnout. The term "burnout" is used to describe a counselor or helper who has been overexposed to pain and is numb. It is as if they do not really have empathy for their clients. This cold, tired, "been there seen that" disconnect from the world has a negative psychological affect on the therapist, the soldier, the therapist's family, and a whole treatment team. Working with people who suffer trauma due to the behavior of others can get anyone feeling angry, disillusioned, and confused. Most kind and caring people are affected by a movie or hearing about a situation where someone got hurt or was unappreciated; the trance thought "that is not fair" is one most of us share.

Those people we are fighting do not talk like us or share many of our central core values and religions. Yet, I have come to see that the villain is our own ambivalence and unresolved issues that come from within. I am not introspective enough nor do I have the patience to figure out when so many of us began to survive our lives instead of live them. I have spent over $50,000 getting a Ph.D. in psychology only to learn that there are many other opinions about our ever-changing world, heads, hearts, and, saddest of all, hopes (Friedman, 1990). That answer I sought was a massive matrix of more questions.

A Call to Service, Bait and Switch

Ambivalence is at the root of the death of close to twenty thousand Americans in the prime of their lives. It was the misinformation about what country should have access to nuclear weapons that let President Bush, suffering from misinformation, put a spin on what was to come. After 9/11/2001, many of us thought we were in a fight for freedom and safety. The ambivalence and guilt of our leaders, and us, and what to do after seven years, can really stir up a lively discussion. Political arguments about what should have happened by who are very unhealthy.

<u>Ambivalence Is the Key to the Baby Steps toward War</u>

The nightly news, daily newspaper, and radio are "too depressing," according to some of my peers working in the medical field. They do not have time to keep up with the "war thing." Acknowledging of their own "denial and avoidance," they discuss life at home and daily distractions. They cannot "keep up with the war, elections, or economics"; life keeps them too busy to follow or even remember we are at war.

I remember how my friends and I in college smoked marijuana and spoke endlessly about "when the revolution comes." Yes, then everything will change! We didn't get out of our pot-induced fog to be agents of change. Many of us were simply oppositional, attending liberal arts university protests and our insight, while grandiose, was that of a big talker observing others blowing up the ROTC building on campus. We sat around waiting for other people to do something! To stay in denial or be distracted by other issues in our lives, we began to see that change would take risk, action, and time. While many of us were big risk takers, we were sadly lacking in focus or energy to facilitate a revolution.

Yes, I admit after reading the amount of trauma research I have compiled for this book *The Unfortunate Hero*, I too felt overwhelmed to see all problems with so few solutions being offered. That is why faith and hope are central to survival.

I have never served in the military or been in combat. It has been through treating survivors torn up by PTSD and loving my spouse and other hurting heroes that I developed my passion to do something, anything, helpful, even with only marginal success that set me on a course to find better solutions for treating addicted soldiers with trauma.

I got sober on June 25, 1983. In the last twenty-five years I have treated thousands of addicted survivors and other dual-disorder individuals. I asked myself, is my calling to develop expertise with military trauma and addiction? To answer that, I would have to refer you to a power greater than myself. In 2006, when I met my military husband, my life changed. We married in 2007. My husband, Sergeant Michael Kelley (retired), spent twenty-two years in the service of our country. For fifteen years he was not in active combat. When the United States deployed our soldiers to the Persian Gulf that changed. Being married to Michael, I observed subtle but powerful fragments as a result of what he saw in the Gulf War and more specifically in Bosnia.

When President Bush deployed many young men and women soldiers to Iraq, those soldiers who were discharged and came home almost immediately were often addicted or suffered from complex PTSD. It was my calling to learn more effective strategies to treat them to stay sober and address coexisting disorders. I have been a consultant to the VA substance abuse treatment program as well as the Department of Defense from the Pacific Rim and throughout the U.S. I admit that I believe I learned as much from those counselors about treating soldiers in the VA system as they learned from my workshops on dual diagnosis. Most of all I learned to honor our soldier hero's by thanking them for serving. And trainers to be sure others remember that the war goes on. In addition this book was written as our attempt to give back even in the smallest way, what they gave up for us.

Secondly, I give of myself as a counselor, writer, and educator what each of us can do to give time, expertise, and friendship to the heroes who have physically been home from war for 40 years or more.

The ideology behind the 12-step programs are to help another addict or alcoholic get and stay sober. Not as a "professional" but as another person who may have marched in their boots.

To avoid burnout as a professional I do my best to take care of myself. Thirty years of giving my heart and mind to hurting survivors has paid its toll on my health. I no longer work 40 plus clinical weeks. At the time of this writing I am in my mid fifties, my stamina and foolishness have both changed...

I used to advise addicted survivors to "take care of themselves." I had forgotten what that mean for me. There is no right answer to this question other than perhaps making your own list of things that help heal your own heart. My list is always being amended but has a grounding in the following:

Pursue daily a stronger relationship spiritually with my God.

Practice spiritual enriching activities such as meditation.

Take time out to go to the doctor when I feel ill.

Laugh!!!

Do not take myself so seriously.

Play with friends, children and grand children.

Learn at least one new thing daily.

Leave a larger tip for a waitress than expected. Anonymous acts of kindness.

Forgive myself and others for not being perfect.

Remember, I would rather be happy than right! Winning an argument on the best way to wash lettuce is not that rewarding!

Work my recovery program one day at a time. Ask for help!

Say "I am sorry, and admit when I am wrong.

Play with children and puppies, you cannot go wrong there!

Evidenced-Based Research Vicarious Trauma

Recently, I was training counselors on how to help our wounded warriors, who come home and ended up alcoholic and addicted to drugs. At the beginning of my training I showed a few minutes of the movie *Stop Loss* (now on DVD). This shows a realistic account of being distracted for only seconds by a cell phone video when soldiers were on patrol. The damage and destruction of this distraction led to death and injury (Chaney and Perlman, 1998).

I am doing research on the counselors attending the training to see if they experienced increased anger and anxiety though exposure to an interview with an unfortunate hero.

Question: Does PTSD lead to vicarious PTSD? The results of this research are staggering, even for those of us who need to be trained and ready to help our wounded soldiers who suffer PTSD and addiction.

It is a fairly well accepted theory that if you hear or see something that is too disturbing to accept you can:

1. Question the source. Where is the research on this issue? It is the intellectual way of putting your fingers in your ears and sticking out your tongue.
2. The second way you can maintain a tight denial system, keeping out all unfriendly thoughts, is to discredit the person telling you what you do not want to hear.

After training sixty-three counselors, all of which had symptoms of PTSD, they self-rated an average of between 7 out of 10. Fifty-eight of the sixty-three had ratings of vicarious PTSD at a 10, the most intense level. Sixty-one out of sixty-three rated experiencing the soldier's pain. I am so thrilled that those therapists were able to be honest and self-monitoring. It will be a huge therapeutic gift when they work with the addicted traumatized soldiers coming home, needing help. (3)

During a recent training, I reviewed the self-rating sheets of all those attending. Out of seventy-nine self-report surveys, 96% of those counselors rated an average of 8 on a 1–10 point scale of their feeling of acute distress of vicarious trauma during the video of the client interview. All rated three or less before driving home (research unpublished K. Evans 2009).

It is common knowledge if you do not like what you are hearing, you either discount the source of the data or the person giving the information. All but one counselor had zero vicarious traumas and added a note written on the feedback sheet to me, "I found the obvious bias of the leader's liberal Democratic view distracting to my ability to learn more about PTSD and the effects, if any, it has on soldiers or therapists." Perhaps, I did say or do something that none of the other seventy-six people in eight trainings noticed. He argued that there was never a stop-loss policy. I have learned to thank people for their input and not debate or take their view as my own. I admit I am liberal and a Democrat. I work with people who need services available mostly through the scarcity of government funding.

The need for many Americans to keep our denial, guilt, or opinions intact requires discrediting me as having knowledge or at least having biased views. I can agree with that. Obviously we all have our own thoughts and feelings. It is part of the gift granted by our Constitution.

I started laughing at the insanity and parody of being too distracted to learn about the distractions of war. I got over my hysterical insight and decided I do think I got some good out of being overly educated. Denial overcomes data when you find the information difficult to accept. Also it would force unwanted change to take in this different information as new facts.

Acceptance with Action

We must accept and expose ourselves to the truth of the collateral damage of this war. A war based on "bad information, misinforming the Americans and Congress that weapons of mass destruction and bin Laden were in Iraq." We invaded Iraq when it is mostly reported that he was in Afghanistan (20, 21, 22). I am sure there are far more complexities here than what I am privy to understand. We all make mistakes. This one cost to date 3.7 trillion dollars. Even with a Ph.D., I do not think that I know how to write that many zeros on a check (5, 6, 22).

Chaos and Confusion Are the Foundation of Traumatic Ambivalence

The term "friendly fire" is used to describe being shot or otherwise injured by a soldier from your own friendly troops. It is a non-enemy injury. To complicate this issue, many "friendly" accidents, bullet or shrapnel wounds, go unreported, as the soldier or the company medic removes it, stitches it up, and the soldier returns to duty. The "suck it up, soldier" military culture redefines what is a true injury. However, I have kept up with percentages of divorce rates, which are getting lower since the January 1, 2010, stopping of stop loss.

This holds true for soldiers' psychological wounds, whose "kill or be killed" survival mentality, a twenty-four-hour hyper-vigilance, creates numerous mental health issues. Being at risk for injury or death as well as observing other soldiers "evaporate" after an improvised explosive device planted under a rock in the middle of a convoy in Iraq, Kuwait, or in the Persian Gulf, is distressing.(4) It is estimated that more than 86% of our troops have symptoms of PTSD from what they have experienced. The vicarious trauma of watching other people being blown up has created extremely high levels of post-traumatic stress disorder.

The *Army Times Magazine* and Military.com report monthly has written a number of articles statistics related to PTSD.(6) I doubt most members of Congress, let alone the average U.S. citizen, subscribes to the military information, which shares the reality of war. Congress argues about whether there is enough money to treat the 650,000 soldiers when they return wounded and forever changed by what they saw and what they did.

The "don't ask, don't tell" policy for defining and reporting being injured on the job differs greatly from that of any private sector employee manual. In simply defining what is standard in terms of what constitutes a soldier's injury, in friendly or unfriendly combat, by the same standard as a typical on the job injury in non-military employment, there would be a dramatic increase of reports. This increased level of friendly fire/injury at work would be headline news. Companies would be shut down. According to several military sources from medic field a unit, only one out of ten non-fatal wounds is even documented. Therefore, what military statistics we could find on non-fatal injuries is inaccurate (7, 13, 21, 22).

Furthermore, if employees working at a company such as Bob's Auto Towing documented a comparative level of non-military injuries similar to the friendly fire accounts, the company would have to close due to the cost of worker compensation rates. That is unless the state or other licensing agencies had not already shut down the company due to an unsafe work environment. In the movie *Stop Loss* the story began with soldiers distracted by looking at text messages on a cell phone. This deadly distraction preceded the horror that followed. This section will discuss three issues uniquely destructive for those who serve in the Iraqi conflict that we can change and must address to prevent further psychological trauma. The issues are:

1) Ambivalence and role confusion. Who am I, soldier or spouse? The next issue of ambivalence is why am I here? What is the point?

2) The betrayal and hostage taking of our own military soldiers through stop-loss.

3) The danger and destruction of the use of instant messaging, cell phones, and email, distracting focus from where they are and creating a longing to be back at home. This no-win situation adds to levels of PTSD fragmentation from ambivalence and survivor guilt.

We live in a world of the desire for instant access to military loved ones. This constant connection is interfering with the focus that our military men and women in Iraq need to stay alert. The hyper-vigilance needed to observe and be ready for unknown life-threatening ambushes and strikes against them is required, if they are to return home unwounded and alive. (8)(9)

Furthermore, the soldier must listen to a sobbing spouse on the phone sharing accounts of missing the soldier so badly that the spouse "can't stand it," the soldier must "try harder to get home sooner." (3) Or hear a guilty confession of a girlfriend's drunken kiss with a stranger in a bar the night before, when out with the girls. "You are the one who enlisted, not me! I get so lonely without your loving." This split of raw emotion of rage, guilt, and fear is destructive to trust and devastating to clear thinking. This split causes dissociation and fragments in the soldier's psychological world. This person needs on-the-spot rehashing and learning how to come out of the trance. He or she can be in only one place at a time, one day at a time. Dissociation refers to when one or more parts of a person are not present. Everyone dissociates when they get distracted from one thing when doing another. A common example of dissociation is forgetting to take a turn or exit when driving, as your mind is elsewhere.

Elsewhere is somewhere between Baghdad and home. That is a huge split of culture, time, and place. If the emotions of the intensity of both locations are strong, it leads to a split of reality as well as priorities and loyalties. Ambivalence, a state of mind with two opposites pulling in two different directions, is one of the most psychologically damaging conditions experienced by the human emotion.

Ambivalence and survivor guilt are key symptoms we need to address to help our wounded warriors as they return home. If they are fortunate to come home, they then suffer conflicts between their roles as spouse and soldier. In our attempts to stay in touch with those we love through text messaging and cell phones, we have endangered their safety. Furthermore, the focus to be 100% soldier is constantly disrupted by complaints of family members who need them at home to help with the kids. The lawn needs mowing. Spouses complain of loneliness and seek the touch of a drinking companion, leading to adultery, guilt, and shame. Yet paradoxically the once-a-week conference calls are very helpful for family members to see and hear that their loved ones are alive and still love them and think about them. It's about timing and balance.

In World War II when a fiancée broke off the relationship, he or she sent a "Dear John letter." All wars have the fear of abandonment by infidelity; it is even reflected in music. The World War II song said, "Don't sit under the apple tree with anyone else but me."

Sadly, a letter written by a girlfriend or wife, declared her inability to "wait for the soldier," selfishly including the details announcing a new hometown love, do not take into consideration the feelings of the man in a war far away. It was a war not started by him, yet one he joined to protect the freedom of the very man who is now with his woman.

The Vietnam war offered much antiwar music through the ambivalence of the culture. Many people today who were not drafted feel guilty for blaming the soldier instead of the war for the horror seen in photographs about the war. The song, "Ruby, Don't Take Your Love to Town," was a strong reminder of the infidelity and emotional abandonment experienced by that era of deployed soldiers.

The "dear John" letter shattered the desire to stay alive. These devastating letters were at least written carefully by hand or typed in complete sentences and sometimes offered an apology. More importantly they were sent through the U.S. mail, and received at mail call, a safe time for reading such devastating news without machine gun in one hand and cell phone in the other.(1)

In today's instant communication, high-speed Internet, cell-phone-crazy world, a text message might say "not n luv with u. Met sum1 nu, luv and sry KT." Imagine if the soldier was out on convoy when this text arrived. The soldier would be so full of hurt and rage, he or she could not focus on the danger ahead. In fact the soldier might fall on a grenade or pipe bomb. Later, his or her "bravery would be commended" as a flag was laid in the lap of an adulterous spouse. This guilt that the spouse or fiancée would live with could become a very destructive family secret.

Perhaps in the family scenario, the soldier does not kill himself. Upon returning home, all is forgiven but not forgotten, or so it seems. The May issue of the *Army Times* magazine reported r several times the rates of deaths and hostile behavior upon return than had been before deployment—self-injury or the injury of others. The quadrupling rate of homicide and suicide among our returning soldiers is shocking. Admirals and health professionals could not account for the increase in the numbers described.

Neither the soldier nor family member is ready for a return home to a world that is one where he or she no longer belongs. The soldier is forever changed with what he or she saw and did. Anger at perceived betrayals and flashbacks combine with reactive, trained responses appropriate to the streets and alleys of Iraq. Anger and rage were needed to keep the adrenaline alive to be able to maintain the mindset of a soldier. These rages of war do not fit well in "polite" society. Living with a running movie of war in his or her brain, the soldier pretends to be numb. The symptoms of PTSD are now escalated by a return to the absence of all the good—he or she thinks, what's the use? The loved ones who begged them to quit the army realize the damage of war on the spouse, now home as per their hysterical demand. The soldier is upset by the confusion and ambivalence of wearing their dog tags under a civilian shirt, now kicked out, separated, and divorced by the one who called the soldier away from his or her military family. Looking in the mirror, the angry drunken stranger is disguised in the body and face that is the soldier's own, forever changed by seeing things that no one should ever see. The soldier feels survivor guilt for leaving early and is also devastated for trying to fight for the Red, White, and Blue only to become an outcast. Unfortunate heroes are imposters in their own minds and hearts. Many called the soldier a "hero," even gave them a hero's welcome. Torn apart inside, lost and alone, the soldier dreams of the brutality of Iraq day and night.(14)

The volunteering for a second or third tour of duty in Iraq takes many traumatized soldiers now disenfranchised and displaced from a place once called home. They go back to the place where they can rage with a gun at an enemy. They can go "blow stuff up"—in Iraq an acceptable behavior. "Who is the enemy? Who is to blame for all of this craziness?" The enemy in Iraq is very difficult to identify. Children are used to carry bombs or as a human shield for a bullet. Those who our military were deployed to invade or rescue know only that there has been more bloodshed since Operation Iraqi Freedom began than before we sent our finest into danger to assist.

The Iraqi people do not welcome of the U.S. soldiers. Pipe bombs carried by children running in narrow streets of Baghdad lead troops into ambush. The blood is shed by all. Both sides of the war give up their lives to a much redefined and confusing cause. CNN has interviewed many Iraq citizens who say there would be far less bloodshed if the U.S. were not there "to help."(15)

These young men and women who enlisted in the military after 9/11 in the belief that they were hunting down bin Laden and his cells of terrorists have been duped. Notice I said women. This the first time in the history of America where women have been trained and deployed into active combat zones, surrounded by the unfriendly, the enemy. I wonder how we got so distracted as to invade Iraq instead of chasing bin Laden into Afghanistan. The soldiers experience ambivalence and fragmentation, and are split in half by the calls from home and tears of fears of loved ones which are in direct conflict with the orders from the military family orders to serve. Then they are told to forget worrying about the family at home, "we are your family here!" One soldier fighting in Baghdad at election time made reference to that "election nonsense." He went on to state that it did not seem to change anything for our soldiers. There was no peaceful withdrawal. Democracy was nowhere, either increased or decreased, just more were lives lost (clinical conversation with a veteran K, Evans 2009).

Generals call for more soldiers, saying a stronger and mightier presence is needed. To respond to the demand for more of a show of force, President Bush initiated the "stop-loss policy." This is often referred to as a backdoor draft. Our troops are comprised of a majority of stop-losses, traumatized, and wounded warriors. Hope for home was high; then new orders: stop-loss. What they thought would be their last dreadful days in Iraq were "stop-loss." Their voluntary enlistment was now an involuntary hostage taking by our own government. Our military took our own troops hostage. The men and women who had already spent years surviving the experience of such unspeakable carnage that they felt lost in their own lives were being held or returned against their will.

The soldier's required mind-set and brainwashing have been broken by the frequency of instant messaging from loved ones. This creates increased levels of ambivalence. This will require special training for those of us who treat their head injury, mental illness, or polytrauma (Friedman, 1990). The recovery process of the effects of polytrauma from military service are complex. The time and intensity of the recovery process involves many issues mentioned previously. To complete recovery and pass the integration goalpost is unrealistic. Soldiers lost by injury, amnesia, or fragmented parts will require weaving PTSD treatment with recovery treatment. They will need to be taught emotional regulation skills to prevent further violence to self and others (Evans and Sullivan 1995).

It will take many years of treatment to reduce PTSD symptoms to a manageable level. We must require participation of all soldiers and their families in a debriefing stabilization-counseling program. We must teach them the symptoms of PTSD, to work with injured brains, which cannot recover if alcohol is used. We all need to listen and understand what is going on within the dark corners of the minds of America's military. We need to stop the promotion of communication via cell phones and text messages that keep our military neither a soldier nor civilian (*Army Times*, April 2008).

If healthcare providers do the job well and are trained to work with the special issues in veterans, the suicide rate may be reduced. We owe those who risked their life and whose families suffered trauma, separation, and divorce a chance to return to a life that is different than the one they left behind.

Do you feel adequately trained to treat our homecoming wounded? The VA has funded outside, private contracts to treat the surge of polytrauma. Jim Benson, Ph.D., a VA psychologist, reported in the *Military Times* that the VA has no experience, knowledge, or success in treating women survivors. Dr. Benson said, "Women just see the world different than men." He went on to say, "We are not trained to know how to help the women soldiers suffering polytrauma returning from duty." He acknowledged the need for training and resources.

Unresolved survivor guilt related to the military or the politics around this war have led to non-military personnel developing vicarious types of trauma, PSD from PTSD. Our soldiers are flooded with survivor guilt and ambivalence. Vicarious trauma is experience by the helper trained to counsel the unique and complex issues related to this war. All Americans and especially therapists in preparing to treat the returning wounded soldiers experience vicarious trauma to some degree. A graduate school study of counselors on identifying vicarious trauma showed 97% of students acknowledged feeling triggered, to some degree, on their own unresolved issues around what happened to the suffering soldiers. They report to be getting outside supervision and further training. I was so impressed with the honesty.

We have collectively numerous clinical skills that will assist vets to diminish their PTSD symptoms (Kennedy and Kelley 2008). However, the hyper-vigilance survivor may misunderstand and add to his or her own survivor guilt if the counselor is unprepared to work with vicarious trauma. Ambivalence is rampant; taking a chance and making any decision is better than no decision at all. We must be ready for deployment as therapists. Be well trained to help the addicted soldiers returning home.

The honored and deserving of America's best heroes deserve funds for counseling, jobs, school, and a home. Upon reentry to the civilian world or before discharge, our heroes will need trained devoted mental health and addiction therapists who can provide counseling that a hero deserves. Vicarious trauma training supervision are just the beginning for our own deployment, as professionals as well as family members I know we all want to effectively provide dual diagnosis services to those who risked their life for our freedom.

To provide consistent love and support to our spouse or other family member Hero, can get rough when the trance states set in, or mood swings come and go before we can even consider how to not react to a negative experience.

Workshops and home study courses that I currently offer are developed from evidence-based practice for treating the "unfortunate hero" and counseling addicted soldier survivors. I invite helpers to call. The soldiers' spouses and loved ones want to help, yet they are co-sufferers and, for the most part, lack training and knowledge, which may lead soldiers and loved ones to feel lost and going in circles. They need our help. There is good reading, blogging and other forms of media out there that can give helpful information. I listed a few sources at the end of this book.

Effects on Families

Trust or the lack thereof has caused divorce and children acting out at home and school. I encourage you to go to the VA, get a Tri-care-approved family therapist and start the transition now. Be sure that the therapist is experienced with the issues of absent parents, grief, and loss.

The damage done by the extended tour is so profound that it can be seen in the lost, dead, staring eyes of a soldier sitting at an airport waiting to redeploy.(30) The betrayal and abandonment from the government, which is then reenacted on family members by broken promises, escalates this deception. Children counted days, marked off in red pen on a calendar, to the day Mommy or Daddy would come home. They came home but then were given stop-loss orders and deployed again. In January 2010, stop loss was stopped. The new commander-in-chief, like many of us, felt that we had not honored our commitment to the soldier, who had showed both honor and valor to us.

Cellular phone calls are bullets to our loved ones. The constant pleas to leave the army are the wounds of lost identity as a soldier. We must stop causing a no-win deep-rooted ambivalence. Treating ambivalence and fragmentation is the key to healing. We will walk through our own vicarious trauma as Americans. We need to ready ourselves to be of service to those whose service was offered freely for us. May all of you find your own path to mentor and guide others to sobriety, spirituality, and a safe road that leads to help understand a new America and a new and different life.

It has been reported by military online reading that many women are deployed soldiers. I will briefly to our female heroes some special issues. I know I am doing a disservice to my sister survivor by not offering more. There are several newly published books that can be found the gives a deeper more effective comment to address some of the treatment needs of this population , including the discussion of the new military code MIS (molested in service), a coding that is approaching 60% of women soldiers according to several sources. This issue is one that may lead many therapists to have strong counter-transference issues. If we are going to be effective in our work with our heroes, we need to wipe our own biases clean and work with the client where there issues begin. Like other trauma therapy, we need outside supervision for transference, which is both healing and destructive. This year, 2010, the movie *The Hurt Locker* won many awards with great admiration. It also demonstrated the third addiction, to adrenaline. We have our work cut out to dissimulate an overactive brain. Your treatment team offers valuable input from all members regardless of education or specialty.

In my first dual-diagnosis hospital we developed during trainings, it was a hostile war between mental health analysts and therapists and twelve-step drug/alcohol counselors. You could cut the tension with a knife. A new administrator was "proof oriented" so we talked, argued, debated, even threatened those with opposing opinions. We were not getting anywhere to resolve the integrated balance needed for good dual-diagnosis treatment. For all managers and doctors, this was self-will run riot. I had not yet learned the fine art of a win/win discussion.

One day I brought a bunch of sponge rubber clown noses to the meeting. Every person wore one as the meeting proceeded. Humor can take down the voltage a long way. Just remember to laugh at yourself. We all are doing the best we can. I sometimes think back on that meeting and wish we had videotaped it.

So what is happening where the professionals are once again disagreeing with basic issues long ago resolved. (Or so I thought). Which came first the chicken or the egg? It is a ridiculous question as there is a chance we could break the egg and eat the chicken. My point is this, your client, or loved one must have integrated dual diagnosis treatment. We cannot bandage a bleeding arm and let a shot leg bleed until we can get to it or until the soldiers dies.

Families, providers, friends and soldiers all want healing and happiness as an outcome. It may take a lot of mistakes to rule out what does not work well so we can find more helpful solutions.

Questions for Chapter 8

1. Have you ever been in a group of people talking and began to feel outraged by someone's statement or comment? What did they say and why do you think it got to you so badly?

2. How do you deal with your irresolvable anger over a situation?

3. When feeling lonely or abandoned what helps you feel better?

4. Are you caught up in a current conflict with someone who makes you feel like you are helpless? What might you try?

Tips for Counselors

There has been a longstanding difference of opinion between mental health training and chemical dependency counselor on the issue of personal sharing of counselor with client. I have heard some heated arguments about boundaries, transference professionalism, and ultimately how much should a counselor share with a client about their personal story. You will see throughout this book at times I share a personal anecdote. I evaluate the appropriateness of counselor sharing through the following criteria:

Is the purpose of my sharing for my client's therapeutic goals or for me to tell a good story?

1. Share generally not specifically enough to achieve clinical goal. Keep good boundaries.
2. Remember that the most effective counselor characteristic to help clients is their ability to be genuine and real.

Chapter 8

Effects of Trauma, Drama, and Addiction on Loved Ones

<u>Ambivalence</u>

I will begin here with what I sometimes think is the basic unraveling of our culture, manners, empathy, and humanness. I like to refer to it as cyber jet lag. When I talk with others about texting instead of talking, email instead of a phone call, or best yet a face to face meeting about important subjects I observe my listener's eyes gloss over. The importance of solid communication, assuring mutual understanding sounds like playing an 8 track tape song version of the newest, fastest and the best recording to date. Yet, I have come to see that the villain is ambivalence, and it comes from within. I am not introspective enough nor do I have the patience to figure out when we all became so narcissistic and began to survive our lives instead of live them.

Once home, veterans have changed and home has changed. Often drinking themselves into oblivion, they end up in jail, a neighbor's yard, kicked out of their home, or with a pistol in their mouth. The abuse of alcohol to numb the pain and turn down the war leads to an increase of flashbacks and dissociative states. Alcohol is also a disinhibitor. That means that the behavior, values and judgments system, whatever little emotional regulation, an individual had is gone. If someone is rude to them or looks at them in a way that is perceived as hostile, there is no ability to control impulses. Judgment went to sleep after three shots of whiskey. In its place entered an angry raging disappointed soldier who is looking for a fight, flight, or freeze (passing out).

Traumatic brain injury has been diagnosed in the first group of medically discharged at the rate of 56%. A damaged brain does not need to be damaged further by using alcohol (Kennedy, Kelly 2008) (Charney and Pearlman 1998). Are but a few researchers estimating that PTSD disables 80% of our active military to some degree. It is a tragedy to resend or redeploy our sick and wounded soldiers back to active duty through an order for stop-loss. No definite release date or time frame is listed.

Stop-loss, a term unknown to many Americans is an outrageous betrayal of those tired warriors who have already served their country. It has been referred to as a back door draft, redeployment without consent. These unfortunate heroes are now prisoners of our own military due to war. Our own military has taken them and held them hostage They did no crime, yet they are doing two and three times the time they enlisted to serve. Promises to family members in letters and by phone that the countdown to the days until home, on everyone's calendar, has just been erased.

The table below represents current deployment strategies.

Phased Implementation of Stop Loss Suspension Component Stop Loss Suspension Date

Active Army	January 1, 2010
Army National Guard	September 1, 2009
Army Reserve	August 1, 2009

Source: Ann Scott Tyson, "Army to Phase Out 'Stop Loss' Practice," *Washington Post*, March 19, 2009.

Military children's trust was lost again when they learned Mommy and or Daddy would not be home when "promised." It was not the intention of a loving deployed parent to lie to a child. The big wall calendar that the child marked off each day until the family would be the same again gets ripped off the wall in a rage of betrayal. A child does not abstract an intellectually twisted concept such as stop loss. They develop a sense of abandonment and begin having nightmares, bed-wetting, and fear of death uncommon to the average eight-year-old. Yet these hurt and angry children are also survivors. They now have their own PTSD and polytrauma from an experience of being lied to, and develop feelings of being hurt, abandoned, and unloved by their solder parent. They now also suffer PTSD symptoms similar to the soldier parent. Vicarious trauma is now the child's reality.

The question asked by many ambivalent and hurting soldiers is, "What was this for? There was no purpose in my being there. I did no good. Nothing changed by my giving years of my life to a war that we have no business involving ourselves in." Furthermore, when they finally do return home, they are no longer the same parents who were deployed to Iraq. In the first ten thousand soldiers returning home, twelve hundred committed suicide waiting to be diagnosed and get treatment from war-related mental, physical, and social abuse.

The VA saw the need to establish a national VA suicide hotline phone number. This was a wise and welcome change in the system of putting individual solders ahead of the military process. Unfortunately, most humans at the point of suicide do not want to call a stranger and discuss their suicidal thinking.

Brain-damaged people forget who they are and where they are. They need a safe and structured environment for recovery, sobriety taught slowly with repetition, and kinetic learning. Touching, art therapy, and role playing are often more helpful tools for the person with frontal brain lobe damage from a learning disability, head injury, or the abuse of alcohol and particularly methamphetamines.

Vicarious trauma touches the lives of those who lose more years from their loved ones as well as all of those who hear the story. The spoils of war also affect the family members of those with loved ones far away. In the transition of the loved ones coming or leaving home, the need to talk about what they saw and did over there is strong. Even if they try to keep it to themselves, they reenact the carnage in daily flashbacks, and they still scream in the night. The bloodcurdling screams or weeping of the soldier who experiences nightmares so common to PTSD awakens a spouse. The struggle to help a loved one through the dissociation, rage, nightmares, and flashbacks brings to a marriage an uninvited intruder. Vicarious trauma and fear for their own safety leads many once loving couples to fight and rage at the ones they love.(20) Ambivalent and lost, the unfortunate hero cannot see him or herself as a good enough soldier or as a good provider with a life career direction once he or she returns home.

How can a single thought be powerful enough to kill? Researchers have demonstrated that ambivalence is killing our soldiers. It is causing a bigger threat to their mental safety than the enemy (terrorists) that they fight, get wounded, and die from. (Charney, A.E., and Pearlman, L.A. (1998).

In addition to this workbook I often use videotaping to help addicted and polytraumatized clients with their permission, I tape a conversation when they appear to be dissociative. I then play the tape for the survivor. I reviewed this information with a soldier I videotaped. He gave me his written consent to use it for workshop therapist counseling or training.

I showed the tape to the soldier. He wanted to see what he looked like when he was dissociated. He wanted to be sure that his support system is aware of this confusion. It was a very helpful intervention for both my client and as part of my counselor-training program.

I got sober on June 25, 1983. In the last two decades I have treated thousands of addicted survivors and other dual-disorder individuals. Many addiction counselors are recovering addicts or alcoholics. Some of these people work at their expense and intuition, and they are the finest counselors I know. I do not think being in recovery itself makes them better counselors, although their passion for learning is a true asset. I worked as a caseworker in mental health before I gave up my Friday night happy hours. I was still very good at using engagement skills. Once sober I found that engagement is the most important skill we need when working as counselors.

I asked myself, "Is my calling to develop expertise with military trauma and addiction? " I pondered this idea of destiny when I divorced my children's father after twenty-five-year marriage. Seven years later I married a retired Army sergeant. I did not have to experience the challenges of military wives during the time that their spouses were deployed. For those spouses reading this, I want to acknowledge that my spouse is a retired Army soldier who served twenty-two years. He does have serious PTSD from Desert Storm. I do believe that a higher power is at work here.

I married Sergeant Michael Kelley after his return from the Persian Gulf, he is changed. Being married to Michael, I observed subtle but powerful fragments of powerful and damaging symptoms of PTSD related to what he saw in the

Gulf War and more specifically Desert Storm. I saw as a new military wife the military and its community from a totally different perspective.

Those soldiers with mental illness and untreated addiction were discharged first and often required my specific specialty. Often due to their addiction or complex PTSD, the soldier broke laws or needed intervention. With exposure to the dangers or potential loss of my beloved spouse, we both saw our calling was to learn more effective strategies to treat them to stay sober and address co-existing disorders

I asked an addicted soldier of the Iraq conflict to allow me to film him while he told his story of his experience during the Iraq war. He shared his level of honesty and hopelessness; he educated me as to what is so different about this war compared to many others. This young man is my stepson Brandon. I did not go out looking for a step-son with PTSD and addiction who just returned home from his deployment. Yet here we all are together talking, crying, laughing, and sharing. I believe that nothing in this world happens by mistake. Yet I have worked with the diseases of addiction and PTSD since I was a college student, long before I got my own help I was reaching out to try to help them. It is very different experiencing something than just reading about it. In the same regard, it takes more than just suffering from a broken leg to know how to fix someone else's leg. Education is required. That is why in 1994, I finally went to graduate school, and by 1999 I was Dr. Katie Evans. Putting the pie together through experience and education is the ideal.

When I interviewed soldiers damaged by this war, at times I feel sick inside. I feel very angry for the lies and deceptions of our own country's leader, which led to scars on so many fine men and women. I suffer what is called vicarious trauma. Simply stated the traumatic information, which I see, hear, treat, or read about, is so disturbing that I will and do have mild symptoms of PTSD (Pearlman and Saarinen 1995).

Evidenced-Based Research on Vicarious Trauma

This led me to do my dissertation on effective methods of engaging, and severing as an agent facilitating change in addicted survivors of trauma. Due to the need for empherical research without too many intervening variables, I needed a sample of clients, to engage in this dual diagnosis model of change I did not have a large enough sample of clients to complete the research with military youth. So I used non military addicted survivors of trauma.

Later I added a piece of exposure of this work through the use of a video. I then included counselor self rating scales of vicarious emotional reactions to secondary trauma this sub study of the phenomena of counselors own emotional reaction. All subjects but one had significant transference about the abuse being discussed. A rating scale was used

Chaos and Confusion

Fortunately in July 2010 a month prior to the military transfers home of soldiers out of Iraq additional funding has been released to a "hero fund" designed specifically to see that deployed and home coming soldier has extra funding for treatment to get medical support. This includes under-funded services, not only mental health and addiction but also dental, and pain management. If we were to keep using the "same don't ask don't tell" defining and reporting of being injured on the job, any private sector employee manual would differ greatly. In simply defining what is standard in what constitutes a soldier's injury, in friendly or unfriendly combat, by the same standard as a typical *on the job injury* in non-military employment, there would be a dramatic increase of reporting.

Thankfully, our culture has changed since Vietnam. When I see soldiers at the airport, I thank them for their service.

Families whose loved ones' ashes and medals on the mantel are all that remains, wonder how did we get so distracted as to invade Iraq instead of chase bin Laden into Afghanistan? Then suddenly, no, the war was not over, as we were needed to help assure the election of a democratic Iraqi president.

The soldier's required mind-set and brainwashing are broken by the frequency of by instant messaging. This level of ambivalence will require special training for those of us who treat their PTSD. Integration of their lost and fragmented parts will require weaving PTSD treatment with recovery treatment, teaching emotional regulation skills to prevent further violence to self and others. (Military Times (May 2008,) Kennedy)

It will take many years of treatment to reduce PTSD symptoms to a manageable level. We must require participation of all soldiers and their families in a debriefing stabilization-counseling program. We must teach them the symptoms of PTSD and to work with injured brains—brains that cannot recover if alcohol is used. We all need to listen and understand to what is going on with in dark corners of the minds of America's military.

This book, *Unfortunate Hero*, is asking who is in charge? Who are now prisoners of our war?

The damage done to the extended tour is so profound that it can be seen in the lost dead staring eyes of a soldier sitting at an airport waiting to redeploy. The betrayal and abandonment from their government and then reenacted on family members by broken promises to family members escalates this deception. Their children's trust was lost again when they said they had to go back. It was not the intention to lie to a child. Yet these hurt and angry survivors are as violated as their soldier parent. Vicarious trauma is now the child's reality. (Pearlman, L.A., and Saarinen, K.W. (1995).

Vicarious trauma touches the lives for those who lose more years from their loved ones as well as all of those who hear the story. The spoils of war also affect the family members of those with loved ones far away. If they are loved, one was able to tell them of their nightmares and pain then the developed vicarious trauma from listening to the near-death experience of their family member or friend. In supporting the transition of loved ones home, the need to talk about what they saw and did over there is strong. Even if they try to keep it to themselves, they reenact the carnage in daily flashbacks, reliving the trauma, they still scream in the night. A spouse is awakened by the bloodcurdling screams or weeping of a spouse as he or she experiences nightmares so common to PTSD. The struggle to help a loved one through the dissociation, rage, nightmares, and flashbacks bring to a marriage an uninvited intruder. Vicarious trauma, fear for one's own safety, leads to many once loving couples fighting and raging at the ones they love. (20) Ambivalent and lost, the unfortunate hero cannot see him or herself as a good enough soldier, or as a good provider with a life career direction upon return home.

In all of my books and writings, I talk about the Karpman triangle. These are concepts from the transactional analysis in the 1970s; it is such simple way to describe the often-complicated dynamics of families and organizations.

The majority of marital disputes are based on issues related to power and control. I have often, in jest, asked the couple I am working with who has more control, and what percentage; they are not to show the slip to their partner. I ask where each person stores his or her control, in a bag or a box? How much space is needed for the storage? I then ask them to show the paper they wrote when we started the exercise. It is at that point we realize control is not a tangible object. It is perception.

The Karpman Drama Triangle

Karpman Triangle

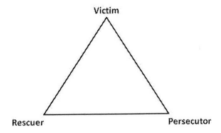

The Karpman triangle is another way to look objectively at the family's dynamics.

Below is a triangle. On one point is the word Persecutor, another point is the word Victim, and lastly, the third point is the Rescuer.

We then ask each person to define what he or she thinks each role reflects. For example, what is a victim? Is a victim someone who is asking for help, takes the help, leaves, and makes changes? You might even get a thank-you card! On the other hand, is a victim someone who doesn't want responsibility for his or her part of the problem or solution? The person wants to nap on the couch and point a finger at the blamer/persecutor for being abusive to them. The victim begs the rescuer to fix things—"Can't you give me money and just fix this?" What is the difference between a helper and a rescuer? Answer: responsibility. If we try to fix the problem, then the victim never learns survivor skills; he or she is always dependent and demanding us to fix it. Pretty soon, you can get frustrated and tired of crisis drama phone calls. Then role changes and the rescuer feels like a victim and gets angry and blames the victim. The triangle below is called the Karpman triangle or the blame game.

We create victims instead of heroes when we try to "fix them"; empowerment to learn the skills for self-help is the key. Sometimes it is frustrating when you have worked hard to support another person and they relapse. Try to detach with lovve and stay off the triangle.

Mental health is about growth, taking responsibility for how you affect others, recognizing choices, and being willing to risk mistakes. The Karpman Drama Triangle is a game played all too often in relationships. If this game defines a pattern of your relationships with others, then you have serious work to do.

Original Source © 1968 by the Transactional Analysis Bulletin.

Here are some tips offered by a group of military wives

Shellie Vandevoorde, Separated by Duty, United in Love (2003, 2006)

The section on departure and the readiness is a quote from Vandevoorde's book

Ways to let service member know you appreciate him or her

1. Never assume they know. Tell them repeatedly how proud you are of them.
2. Let them know you miss their personal involvement with the kids.
3. Let them know you miss "just talking" with them.
4. Let them know you respect their honor and loyalty to our country.
5. Reassure them that you will be strong and maintain the home front.
6. Acknowledge little "honey do's" they did for you before deployment.
7. Discuss future family outings that entire family will enjoy.

Tips to Remember

1. Do not test your relationship with infidelity.
2. Set aside time before the deployment to discuss fidelity in your relationship.
3. Hang around with friends who are at the same level or higher in a relationship as you are.
4. Be aware that time apart will often make the relationship stronger and more meaningful.
5. Decide which is worse: knowing or not knowing the truth.
6. Love is not just an emotion, but also loyalty and a vow.
7. Remember, if you believe your marriage is worth the effort to save, and then it probably is.
8. Seek counseling. Many resources are available to help. Do not hesitate to talk with a professional.

9. Do not kid yourself; when tension exist between Mom and Dad, children can feel it.
10. Use marital aids if you want. They can be useful in long-distance relationships.

Another book I found that might be helpful to newly married wives is the book, *Married to the Military*, written by a group of wives (main author Meredith Leyva, published in 2003 by Fireside). It gives very simple tips on the how it is to marry the military. This is a basic introduction to military routines, medals, ribbons, and the basics of military life.

I am thankful for the women who offered us tips from their own experiences. Do you feel adequate and ready for the homecoming of your loved one? Do you have unresolved survivor guilt related to the military or the politics around this war? Our soldiers are flooded with survivor guilt and ambivalence.

Our heroes are finally leaving Iraq much later than promised; they will have issues with trust. If the soldier had childhood abandonment, neglect, abuse, or infidelity during deployment, a therapeutic alliance will take special clinical knowledge. It is just the beginning for our deployment to effectively provide dual-diagnosis services to those who risked their lives for our freedom.

My workshops and home study courses on evidenced-based practice for assisting other counselors in learning some of the special treatment thoughts appear in this book. The rest of this book is dedicated to the military and their families to read to offer hope, honor, and knowledge from the "Unfortunate Hero: Counseling addicted soldier survivors." I am training the trainers and invite them to call me so I can share more with them as we all learn together how to do our best for loved ones and volunteers. Unfortunate heroes, you can begin to trust again. You can talk with your loved ones. You and they never need to feel lost, alone, invisible, or like a wounded dog or an unfortunate hero.

Chapter 9

Faith and Fear, Now a Fortunate Hero

I have heard it said many times that it is impossible to feel a strong sense of trust and faith in God and suffer from fear at the same time. I have found that to be true. Prior to getting clean and sober in 1983, I never felt at peace. I thought I was in, or should try to, control everyone and everything. I used to tell my friends in regards to my work as child protective service worker, "If people would just do what I say, everything would be just fine!" That was the thinking that led me to take Valium to stay calm when stressed at work or get seriously drunk one weekend a month.

It was hard for me to accept that I was alcoholic. I had cut down and developed a complex list "of rules" to prevent me from becoming an alcoholic, like my mother, brother, and father. The Alcoholics Anonymous Big Book (World Service Center) has a chapter where it discusses "ways we tried to control our drinking." I had entered treatment to detoxify off Valium.

I argued with counselors. "I have done my share of drinking and using drugs. I went to the University of Oregon, known for its liberal nature including liberal use of marijuana. But I quit illegal drugs when I got out of college and became a professional." I could not see that the daily use of Valium I took prescribed by my family doctor was a problem; he never said anything about refills. I only went to one doctor for my medicine. As it turned out, this doctor ended up in treatment and recovery several years after I did.

I will always be grateful to those counselors who put up with my denial. I could say I was an addict; after all, I was in DTs. But I did not want to be an alcoholic like my other family members. My parents drank daily; my father, mother, and brother all had a dual diagnosis. My mother suffered major depression and tried to drink it away, my brother was bipolar and a polytrauma drug dependent, my father suffered symptoms of PTSD from World War II until the day he died. He tried to drink away the feelings and "nervousness" along with nightmares, night terrors, night sweats, and waking up due to all the physical pain he suffered from back surgery, war injuries and several strokes. The five years prior to my parents and brothers death, all four of us were clean and sober and active in twelve-step programs. It was a real tear jerker on my parents' sobriety birthday for those in the room who still had parents active in their disease or who died drunk. This is just one of the many blessings I have from God, the twelve-steps and recovery.

One of the co-founders of Alcoholics Anonymous stated in an unpublished writing that he thought, "Alcoholics are born with an emptiness, a separation between man and God. As a result of this empty feeling we try to fill it with alcohol. We give the power and control of our life to idolatry, the bottle became our God."

Spirituality is not a religion. Religions do offer spirituality. Many addicts are resistant to attending twelve-step programs since they heard from someone in a bar it as a religion. They are often angry at a God that would allow bad things to happen to good people, or they have unresolved issues with childhood church that need to be discussed.

The twelve-step programs discuss finding a God of your understanding. This is not meant to be sacrilegious, nor is it meant to throw anyone into a philosophical spin. It simply means find a power greater than yourself. After all, you got yourself drunk. It could be God: Group Of Drunks or Good Orderly Direction. It is important to get this. We alcoholics are trying to control the world and do not trust that things will get better one day at a time.

In graduate school I did my dissertation on conversion experiences: What makes survivors with PTSD and addiction change? After two years of research of the seven main religions of the world compared to the twelve-steps I discovered that they were far more alike than different.

The central theme in what I read was this: "There is a God and it is not me!" This means that success and happiness can be found by having faith, being kind to others, and doing the best you can. No one among us knows it all or will ever be perfect. If we could get to a place where we could realize that ultimately we have to choose, "Would I rather be right or happy?" We might find true bliss. An Eastern religion quotes Buddha as saying, "What you own owns you." This addresses our mistaken desire to have more stuff to be happy. St. John in the Bible says God is love. Many new age or new thought Christians believe we need to put good in and good will come back to us three fold.

In the appendix section of this book, I inserted a copy of the Twelve Steps. In addition I included a simple shaman belief structure called the Four Agreements. These are two different spiritual wisdoms that can help with not only getting sober but getting happy and building self-esteem. When I was able to follow these simple rules of thumb I found I accidently got happy!

Many of us, myself included, try to be perfect, right, never make a mistake. This thinking drove me into detox. It is progress not perfection. Have faith and do the next right thing.

I can only hope that this book is useful to you. Perhaps help you on your own path to recovery.

I share this with all of you in hope that it will offer some guidance away from the pain and fear and that you will come to believe as Michael and Brandon have that the imperfection in their pain is an opportunity for you or another Unfortunate Hero.

If you have felt like defective human, or to quote my stepson Brandon, a "wounded dog," I hope the sharing of our knowledge and experience helps take you one step further on your path of recovery as a fortunate hero. I have found that survivors are the most interesting and gifted people I have ever met. Look for the hero in you. Maybe we will see you on the path of recovery. Michael and I will be traveling doing workshops, meetings and signing these books.

If you wish to reach us, go to my website at www.drkatieevans.com for contact information.

Appendix and Updates

The Twelve Steps

1. We admitted we were powerless over alcohol—that our lives had become unmanageable.

2. Came to believe that a power greater than ourselves could restore us to sanity.

3. Made a decision to turn our will and our lives over to the care of God *as we understood him.*

4. Made a searching and fearless moral inventory of us.

5. Admitted to God, to us, and to another human being the exact nature of our wrongs.

6. Were entirely ready to have God remove all these defects of character.

7. Humbly asked him to remove our shortcomings.

8. Made a list of all persons we had harmed, and became willing to make amends to them all.

9. Made direct amends to such people wherever possible, except when to do so would injure them or others.

10. Continued to take personal inventory and when we were wrong promptly admitted it.

11. Sought through prayer and meditation to improve our conscious contact with God *as we understood him,* praying only for knowledge of his will for us and the power to carry that out.

12. Having had a spiritual awakening as the result of these steps, we tried to carry this message to alcoholics, and to practice these principles in all our affairs.

Don Miguel Ruiz
Offers us the four agreements as a simple Mexican Shaman's advice for a happy life

The Four Agreements

Be impeccable with your word.
Don't take anything personally.
Don't make assumptions.
Always do your best.

Military Divorce Statistics

According to Department of Defense statistics, in the past ten years, the military divorce rate has steadily grown. During the fiscal year 2006 and 2007, it was 3% while in 2008 it became 3.4%.

Military Divorce Statistics in different services

Services	Overall Divorce Rate	Officer Divorce Rate	Enlisted Divorce Rate
Army	3.5	2.3	3.9
Air Force	3.5	1.6	4.1
Navy	3.0	1.5	4.1
Marine Corps	3.5	1.6	3.5

Military Divorce Statistics of the Sexes

Services	Male Divorce Rate			Female Divorce Rate		
	2006	2007	2008	2006	2007	2008
Army	2.5	2.6	3.0	7.9	8.1	8.5
Air Force	2.6	2.9	2.9	6.2	6.5	6.5
Navy	2.9	2.8	2.5	6.9	6.5	6.3
Marine Corps	2.9	3.0	3.2	7.1	8.1	9.1

2005 witnesses a drop in statistics

In 2004, the military divorce rate spiked up. During this year, 3,325 army officers opted for divorce and the number of enlisted members who got divorced was 7,152. The military personnel were offered new and beefed up programs in 2005. The effect was remarkable and the divorce rate plummeted by 61%. In 2005, 1,292 army officers and 7,075 enlisted members got divorced. If the officer corps were taken into consideration, 6% of married officers divorced in 2004 while in 2005, this figure was 2.3%.

Efforts to decrease divorce statistics

The U.S. military has introduced programs with the intention of providing assistance to military families to bear the hardships of life. For example, there are weekend retreats for military couples and support groups for spouses of deployed personnel. Such programs are made available through mental health and family support counseling networks.

Some of the attempts made by the army to decrease divorce statistics are as follows:

- The PICK (Premarital Interpersonal Choices and Knowledge) is a partner program to enable single soldiers to make astute decisions to select their life mate.
- The Strong Bonds Marriage Education Program is related primarily to issues that have an impact on reserve and National Guard couples.
- The Building Strong and Ready Families Program. The intention of this program is to enhance the communication skills among the married partners. This is a two-day program that is reinforced by a weekend retreat.
- The Military OneSource Program aims to maneuver soldiers and families to resources that would support them.
- A family support group system offers emotional and practical support to spouses of deployed soldiers.
- The Deployment Cycle Support Program makes soldiers aware of how family relations are affected by their absence and return and how the soldiers can adjust to the unavoidable changes.

Some facts and hope

- Among active-duty army officers and enlisted personnel, the divorce cases doubled from 5,658 to 10,477 from 2001 to 2004. Some officials believe this increase might be due to the stress of deployment.
- The possibility that the marriage of enlisted service members would end in a divorce is more than for officers, and this may be taking place because enlisted service members are younger.
- As compared with men, women in each military service are two times more likely to opt for divorce. It has been proved after some research that the current programs in the military offer very little support for spouses and families.
- You do not need to be a statistic, after all you are a Hero!

Original Source © *2010* www.edivorcepapers.com/divorce-statistics/military-divorce-statistics.html

Sources and Bibliography

(1) Friedman, M.J. (1990). Interrelationships between biological mechanisms and pharmacotherapy of post-traumatic stress disorder. Dissociative mechanisms in post-traumatic stress disorder. In M.E. Wolf and A.D. Mosnaim (Eds.). Post-traumatic Stress Disorder: Etiology, Phenomenology, and Treatment. Washington, DC: American psychiatric Press.

(2) Charney, A.E., Pearlman, L.A. (1998). The ecstasy and the agony: The impact of disaster and trauma work on the self of the clinician. In P. Klee spies (Ed.), Emergency psychological services: The evaluation and management of life-threatening behavior, pp. 418–435. New York: The Guilford Press

(3) Hoffman, Michael (2008). Jamie's war wounds. Army Times Magazine, pp. 28–30.

(4) Cole, P.M., and Putman, F.W. (1992). Effects of incest on self and social functioning: A developmental psychopathology perspective. Journal of Consulting and Clinical Psychology, 60. pp. 174–184. Diagnostic and Statistical Manual of Mental Disorders, (4th Ed.). (1994) American Psychiatric Association, Washington, DC.

(5) Gorski, T. (1982). Counseling for relapse prevention. Independence, MO: Herald House

(6) Kennedy, Kelly (2008). Rand report shows PTSD, TBI could cost the nation billions. <u>Army Times Magazine,</u> April 28, p. 27

(7) Kennedy, Kelly (2008). Study: Group therapy helps troops with combat stress. <u>Army Times Magazine</u>, July 28, pp. 26–27

(8) Kennedy, Kelly (2008). Vet's group: claims DoD violates severance law. <u>Army Times Magazine</u>, June 30, p. 16

(9) Kennedy, Kelly (2008). Vets groups, VA back bill to boost family counseling. <u>Army Times Magazine</u>, July 7, p. 13

(10) Keyser, Sharon (2008). A welcome home for every warrior. <u>Army Times Magazine</u>, May 12, p. 6.

(11) Kennedy, Kelly (2008). Lawmakers advocacy groups criticize vets disability bill. <u>Army Times Magazine</u>, April 21, p. 18

(12) Addendum H: Soldier and Family Action Paper, <u>2008 U. S. Army Posture Statement</u>.

(13) Briere, J., and Runetz, M. (1987). Post-Sexual Abuse Trauma: Data and Implications for Clinical Practice. <u>Journal of Interpersonal Violence</u>, 2, 4, pp. 367–379.

(14) Ellenson, G. S. (1986). Disturbance of Perception in Adult Female Incest Survivors: Social Casework. <u>Journal of Contemporary Social Work</u>, 67, pp. 149–159.

(15) Brown, J.M., and Miller, W.R (1993). Impact on motivational interviewing on participation and outcome in residential alcoholism treatment. <u>Psychology of Addictive Behaviors</u>, 7, p. 211–218

(16) McMichael, William H. (2008). GAO study: More sex assaults occur than are reported. <u>Army Times Magazine</u>, April 14, pp. 12–13.

(17) Maze, Rick (2008). Tale of lost files highlights problem with VA records. <u>Army Times Magazine</u>, April 14, p. 34.

(18) Veterans Administration Fact Sheets May 2008 www. Military.com

(19) McMichael, William H. (2008). Mullen supports shorter tours, but says stress hard to gauge. <u>Army Times Magazine</u>, April 14, p. 20.

(20) Veterans Administration Fact Sheets March 2008 www. Military.com

(21) Tan, Michelle (2008). Stuck on Stop-Loss. <u>Army Times Magazine</u>, May 5, p. 8

(22) <u>Here are some tips offered by a group of military wives</u> Shellie Vandevoorde, Separated by Duty, United in Love (2003, 2006)

(23) Pearlman, L.A., and Saarinen, K.W. (1995). <u>Trauma and the therapist: Counter transference and vicarious traumatization in psychotherapy with incest survivors</u>. New York: W.W. Norton

(24) Meredith Leyva published in 2003 by Fireside

(25) Karpman Triangle (Original Source © 1968 by the Transactional Analysis Bulletin. Adapted by Evans and Sullivan).

(26) <u>On Killing</u>, David Grossman, 1976, 2006 2nd Ed. Back Bay Books, New York, New York)

11257500R00120

Made in the USA
Charleston, SC
10 February 2012